Walks For All Ages
NORFOLK

WALKS *FOR* ALL **AGES**

NORFOLK

SARAH JUGGINS

BRADWELL
BOOKS

Published by Bradwell Books
9 Orgreave Close Sheffield S13 9NP
Email: books@bradwellbooks.co.uk

1st Edition
Reprinted 2017

ISBN: 9781910551738

Print by: Gomer Press, Llandysul, Ceredigion SA44 4JL

Design by: Andy Caffrey

Typesetting by: Mark Titterton

Photographs: All images the author except

© Holkham Estate on page 47
© Borough Council of King's Lynn & West Norfolk on pages - 12/13
Mark Titterton on pages - front cover; 2, 6; 55; 62/63
iStock on pages - 9;10; 11; 72; 73; 75; 77; 78/79
Geograph – creative commons on pages - 27 R Humphrey; 28 A S Pye; 34 A Dace;
35 K Walters; 36 N Mutton; 64 C Tuck; 69 G Hughes; 85 E Simak; 89 E Simak;
93 t G Denny & b G Denny; 94 t G Denny

Maps: Contain Ordnance Survey data

© Crown copyright and database right 2017

Ordnance Survey licence number 100039353

CONTENTS

INTRODUCTION

SITTING ON THE EASTERN EDGE OF THE UK, NORFOLK IS A COUNTY WITH A DIVERSE MIX OF LANDSCAPES AND A LARGELY RURAL POPULATION. THE NORTH SEA LAPS AT ITS COAST, RESULTING IN A SOMETIMES WILD AND BLEAK LANDSCAPE, WHILE INLAND THE COUNTY IS CHARACTERISED BY ROLLING FIELDS, SCATTERED WOODLANDS, TREE-LINED COUNTRY ROADS AND TRADITIONAL, SMALL VILLAGES.

There are four major cities or towns: the capital city of Norwich, the holiday destination Great Yarmouth and the towns of King's Lynn to the west of the county and Thetford to the south. Other smaller, market towns such as Wymondham, North Walsham, Downham Market and Swaffham tend to burst into life on market days.

There has been a tendency for people to dismiss Norfolk as a flat, agricultural county, which is as far from the reality as it is possible to get. North Norfolk has rolling hills that lead from the spectacular coastline into the heathlands that lie back from the sea. The

dunes along the eastern seaboard near Cromer and Great Yarmouth rise magnificently into the sky. Norwich has the distinction of having more hills than any other city in England, while all over the county hidden lanes, well-used ancient walking ways and quiet country roads meander through and roll over the countryside.

There is nothing uniform about this county. Norwich is a bustling, vibrant, hipster city, with a large selection of independent shops, ancient buildings and modern architecture; King's Lynn is an intriguing mix of history and beauty combined with urban decay. Then there are the villages: flint and the local carrstone are the predominant building materials and, with Norfolk being one of the driest and sunniest counties in England, the villages are usually decorated with a splash of colour as flowerbeds, hedgerows and roadsides are bursting with flowers, trees and bushes.

The countryside can be divided into four main areas. The Norfolk Broads are a well-known phenomenon, a watery network of rivers and lakes on the eastern side of the county. The Brecks offers a unique landscape to the south of the county. Purple heathers, yellow gorse and wind-twisted pines make this a landscape from another era.

The coastline of north Norfolk stretches from Snettisham to Cromer and is a mix of wide, sandy beaches such as Holkham and Brancaster or the pebbled, steeply climbing beaches of Cley and Salthouse. The beaches are backed up by dunes, pine forests or marshlands. The Norfolk Coastal Path takes in this beautiful landscape, which at a sunset or sunrise can be truly mesmerising.

The fourth landscape that you encounter in Norfolk is the Fens to the north-west of the county. This is the black, flat landscape that has resulted from man reclaiming land from the sea. Lacking the more natural beauty of the rest of the county, this is still a remarkable and evocative landscape that deserves to be explored.

Some of the walks in this book follow country lanes and roads, when following these routes please remember the advice given in the Highway Code for pedestrians when there is no pavement.

Keep to the right-hand side of the road so that you can see oncoming traffic. You should take extra care and be prepared to walk in single file, keep close to the side of the road.

1 KING'S LYNN – TOWN WALK

BRIM FULL OF HISTORY AND WITH A VIBRANT TOWN CENTRE, KING'S LYNN IS THE MAIN TOWN IN WEST NORFOLK. ITS HANSEATIC HISTORY MEANS THAT KING'S LYNN WAS ONCE ONE OF ENGLAND'S MOST IMPORTANT PORTS FROM AS EARLY AS THE 12TH CENTURY AND THIS MARITIME PAST IS STILL VERY MUCH IN EVIDENCE TODAY.

Fine old merchants' houses stretch down to the river between cobbled lanes, and the elegant Custom House overlooks the harbour. The town's heritage is reflected in an amazing array of historic buildings and its two magnificent marketplaces: Saturday Market Place, where St Margaret's Church, designated as a Minster Church in 2011 by the Bishop of Norwich, is surrounded by splendid buildings, and Tuesday Market Place, quite possibly one of England's grandest squares, with its imposing Georgian facades.

Once known as Bishop's Lynn, King's Lynn was renamed by Henry VIII. Its turbulent religious past is still in evidence in the shape of Whitefriars, Blackfriars and Greyfriars Tower – three monasteries built by Carmelite, Dominican and Franciscan monks respectively. Of the three, the arch at Whitefriars and the Tower at Greyfriars remain and can be seen on this walk.

These days, King's Lynn is working hard to re-establish ties with the maritime towns of the Baltic and North Sea. In the 13th century, King's Lynn was one of England's great maritime centres and the UK's first member of The Hanse – a network of coastal towns and cities whose main trade and culture revolved around their ports.

Members of Die Hanse, as it was known, created the Hanseatic League, a network enabling members to trade, communicate and develop other social and commercial links. In recent years, the Borough Council and local historical organisations have worked hard to re-build and reconnect with the original members of the Hanseatic League. There are currently four members in the UK – King's Lynn, Aberdeen, Edinburgh and Hull – and references and information about the League are to be found throughout the town centre and port area.

Before any visitor is lulled into thinking that King's Lynn is an idyllic market town, it must be pointed out that it is also in one of the most impoverished postcodes in the UK. This walk will take you through the beautiful, historic centre, along the pretty quayside but also past some of the poverty-stricken housing estates. It is a typical example of a town and population that can be found on the extremities of the UK.

THE BASICS

Distance: 4 miles / 6km

Gradient: Easy

Severity: Easy

Approx. time to walk: 2½ hours

Stiles: None

Map: OS Explorer 236 (King's Lynn, Downham Market & Swaffham)

Path description: Minor roads, urban centre, cobbled road, some unpaved paths, grassy tracks

Start point: Lynn Sport (Alive Leisure) (GR TF 632210)

Parking: Alive Leisure car park (PE30 2NB)

Dog friendly: There is traffic all along this route so keep dogs on a lead

Public toilets: Tuesday Market Place, The Walks

Nearest food: The Dukes Head, Tuesday Market Place; the Market Bistro, Saturday Market Place, plus cafes and shops along the route

1 KING'S LYNN – TOWN WALK

The Route

1. From the car park at Alive Leisure, head towards the leisure centre buildings. Take the tarmac path to the right, which takes you past the athletics track to your left and the Shed Skateboard Centre to your right. Follow the path to the river and then turn right along the marked footpath. Follow the path as it tracks the course of the river. Ignore the first turning on your right and take the second. Continue to follow the footpath over the footbridge and through an underpass.

2. Where the river meanders around to the left, follow the footpath that takes you right. Follow the path until it emerges onto Loke Road. Turn left and follow the footpath to the top of the road. This is John Kennedy Road. There is a pedestrian crossing a few metres to your right. Use this and then turn left towards the old town. Turn right into North Street.

   Cross North Street by the traffic lights. After about 25 metres turn right along a narrow passageway. Follow the cobbled street past old houses on the left and St Nicholas' Chapel on the right.

3. Turn into Austin Street. Opposite are the remains of the gateway of the Augustine Friary (1293-1539). Turn right and shortly turn right at the 'T' junction heading towards the chapel. At the junction, turn left along St Nicholas Road into the Tuesday Market place.

4. Turn left and go towards the Dukes Head Hotel. Make your way across the square towards the Globe Hotel – this is diagonally opposite where you entered the market square. Turn left along King Street towards the Custom House. Just before the Custom House turn right to go past the statue of Captain George Vancouver (1759–1798). At the riverside turn left over the Purfleet Bridge and follow the riverside quay. After 200 metres, turn left along College Lane. You will emerge onto the Saturday Market Place by St Margaret's Church. Head straight up St James Street and after 400 metres you will see Greyfriars Tower. Turn right down Tower Place and right again down Millfleet. At the small roundabout take the right-hand turn down Church Street which leads you back to the Saturday Market Place.

   Once you have returned to the Saturday Market Place, turn left along St Margaret's Place and into Nelson Street. At Mill Fleet turn right past the Greenland Fishery – this is thought to be one of King's Lynn's oldest buildings. Where the road bears left, stay straight on to pass the remains of Whitefriars. Follow this road, which turns into a grassy track, as far as the Southgates – the remains of the old town wall.

5. Turn left along London Road and cross over at the statue of Frederick Savage, former mayor of King's Lynn. Walk down Guanock Terrace as far as Exton's Road and the entrance to the Walks, a large public park. Go into the Walks and stay on the path straight ahead, which takes you past the Red Mount Chapel. Where the path ends, turn right and follow until you come to a railway crossing. Cross here and turn immediately right down a cycle path. This is signposted to Alive Leisure/ Lynnsport. Follow the path back to the car park, taking care as you cross the main Gaywood Road.

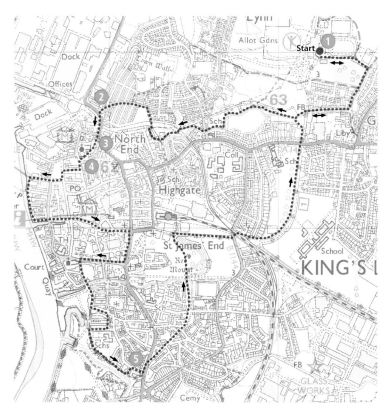

Photographs: © Borough Council of King's Lynn & West Norfolk

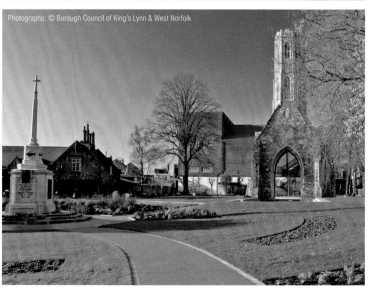

2 CASTLE RISING

CASTLE RISING HAS A MAGNIFICENT NORMAN CASTLE, AND IS A VILLAGE WITH AN AIR OF HISTORIC IMPORTANCE ABOUT IT. IN FACT, THIS WALK WILL ALSO PROVE THAT IT IS SET IN AN ENVIRONMENT THAT IS IMPORTANT FOR ITS RICHNESS AS WELL AS IT DIVERSITY.

Ancient woodlands, mineral-rich soil, babbling brooks, open fields and grassy, well-trodden tracks combine to make this a fascinating wander through lovely English countryside. The village itself, just off the main A149, is a traditional Norfolk village with carrstone (red sandstone) cottages, historic almshouses, a popular pub – the Black Horse – and a fascinating history. Who could want more?

Castle Rising's most famous historical resident was the power-hungry wife of Edward II. One account suggests that Isabella – also known as the She-Wolf of France, which gives a clue to her personality – helped her lover, Roger Mortimer, murder her husband. Isabella then ruled the country for the next few years in the name of her 15-year-old son, who was crowned Edward III on his father's death.

Once Edward III reached maturity it was clear something had to be done to keep his mother out of affairs of state and so she was sent from London to live in a number of country houses and castles – one of which was Castle Rising.

With the monarch's mother in residence, Castle Rising went through a makeover, with stories about a number of carpenters and builders being shipped in to make the castle impressive enough for the Dowager Queen. Isabella is known to have resided at Castle Rising for many months of each year from 1331 until her death in 1358, and was visited by the King on a number of occasions. She always brought an army of servants, and archaeological evidence has revealed that a lot of building work was carried out during the years Isabella took up residence. As you walk around the edge of the castle today, it takes some imagination to picture the sleepy village as a hub of royalty and court life.

The castle has a great deal to offer, starting with its awesome banks and ditches, its half-buried Norman chapel and its two wells. But the most impressive feature is the keep, a squat, rectangular tower that stands some 50 feet (15m) high. The blind arcading (a series of arches on a wall) that decorates its front would not be out of place on a grand cathedral and helps to make this one of the finest castles in England.

THE BASICS

Distance: 6 miles / 9.5km

Gradient: Nearly all flat

Severity: Quite easy

Approx. time to walk: 2½ hours

Stiles: None

Map: OS Explorer 250 (Norfolk Coast West)

Path description: Marked trails and footpaths, one slightly boggy part by the river

Start point: Castle Rising car park (free) (GR TF 666245)

Parking: Castle Rising car park (PE31 6AH)*

Dog friendly: Yes, but be aware of animals and nesting birds

Public toilets: At start of walk

Nearest food: Cafe as you finish the walk, just 100 metres on the right before you return to the car park

*NB Be aware that from November to March the car park closes at 4pm

2 CASTLE RISING

The Route

1. Leave the car park and turn left towards the village. At the crossroads go straight across the road past the small complex of shops, which includes a cafe and tea room. After  approximately 200 metres you will see a turning on your right, which takes you onto a minor track. Follow this for about half a mile. There is a conservation area on your left, where many native British species have been planted, and a plantation on your right. Continue along the path until you reach the A149.

2. Taking great care as this is a busy road, cross the A149 and follow the footpath directly opposite. This track winds through the trees, and can get wet and muddy at times. You will cross a small brook, which can be orange in colour – this is the effect of dissolved iron-rich rocks under the surface. Eventually you emerge at a small group of houses. Take the path  straight ahead of you, ignoring the path that turns sharply to your right. This path takes you through woods until you emerge through a metal gate onto open fields.

3. Veering right, the footpath will lead you to a track that follows the course of the Babingley River. Keep the river on your left as you navigate across the fields and over two stiles. Be aware that farm animals do graze here, so keep dogs under control at all times.

4. When you get to the point where the field ends, leave the riverside and turn right. After 100 metres you will come to a double gate and a stile. Turn left onto a tarmac road. At the junction turn right and follow the road towards Roydon.

5. After just under a mile, you will come to the A148. Cross this with care and follow the road for another three-quarters of a mile until you see All Saints Church on your right-hand side. It is worth stopping for a look at the church, with its impressive Romanesque south door.

(If you want to stop for a coffee or lunch, the Three Horseshoes is a nice pub in the heart of Roydon. To reach the Three Horseshoes, continue straight past the church on Station Road until you see a left-hand turn onto Low Road. Follow this

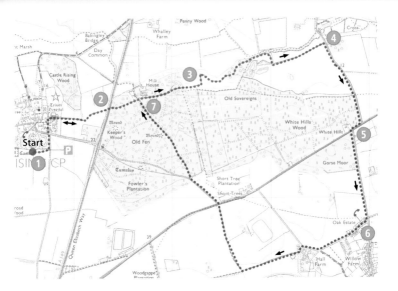

to Lynn Road, where you will find the pub. The pub is approximately three-quarters of a mile from the church, so a detour will add a mile and a half to your journey.)

6. Resuming the walk from All Saints Church, follow Church Lane as it swings around to the left. After approximately three-quarters of a mile, you will see a turning on your right-hand side with a farm and a veterinary clinic. Take the track to the right of these buildings and follow the track. Where you reach a junction, turn right and follow the track up a slight incline. The track winds to the left before eventually meeting the A148. Cross the road and follow the minor tarmac road, which is lined with ancient trees. After quarter of a mile, you will see a turning into the forest on your right. Follow the marked footpath as it winds through the forest. You will be walking through conservation land on either side, so keep to the footpath.

7. Eventually you will emerge back at the small settlement you passed through earlier. Keep to the left of the buildings and follow the track back through the woodland. You will emerge onto the A149; cross over here and retrace your footsteps back along the footpath into the village. As you reach the road, turn left towards the castle and car park.

3 ROYDON COMMON

THIS WALK TAKES YOU OVER THE TWO ADJOINING AREAS OF HEATHLAND, ROYDON COMMON AND GRIMSTON COMMON. IT IS A BEAUTIFUL, MELANCHOLIC LANDSCAPE WHERE, IF YOU ARE LUCKY, YOU WILL SEE A MULTITUDE OF WILDLIFE.

It is also a landscape that can look entirely different dependent upon the season. In winter it is stark, as the trees stand out in sharp silhouette against the expansive skies; in spring, the gorse adds a flash of yellow and gold, while summer and autumn is a riot of changing colours as the heather, flowers and trees all go through their cycles.

The heathland in this area of west Norfolk is a great example of conservation in action. Since 1800, more than 75 per cent of England's heathlands have been lost to farming, housing developments and other uses, so preserving this site has become of great importance in the battle to preserve some of our natural habitats. The process of regenerating heathland is ongoing and the process can be seen over the course of this walk.

Roydon Common has been under the protection of Norfolk Wildlife Trust (NWT) – the oldest wildlife trust in the UK – since 1963. In 1999, NWT bought 40 acres of neighbouring land, which had originally been heathland but was now planted with conifers.

The land was cleared and the land restored to its original state with heather, gorse and other heathland plants flourishing. The work has resulted in the return of many native plants and birds, in particular the nightjar and the woodlark. The heathland plants have grown from seeds that lay dormant for years but which germinated as soon as the conifers were felled.

Now the same process is happening on the adjacent Grimston Common. In 2004, NWT launched a major appeal to buy 69 acres of conifer-covered land. The appeal was successful and the conifers have since been felled and the land is slowly returning to its natural state.

The management of the large heathland area is helped by nature. Rare breeds are used to maintain the restored heath, particularly Dartmoor ponies and Hebridean sheep, which roam wild across the 109 acres. In particular, these animals keep the invasive birch and bracken at bay.

Wildlife is benefitting hugely from the restoration. Besides the nightjar and skylark, visitors can also spot bees, dragonflies, reptiles, amphibians, and an array of brightly coloured butterflies and moths. There are also brown hares, roe and fallow deer, kestrels, buzzards, harriers and merlins.

THE BASICS

Distance: 5½ miles / 8.75km

Gradient: Some slight inclines

Severity: Quite easy

Approx. time to walk: 2½ hours

Stiles: Two – dog friendly

Map: OS Explorer 236 (King's Lynn, Downham Market & Swaffham)

Path description: Marked trails and footpaths, one slightly overgrown stretch on the disused railway line

Start point: Roydon Common car park (GR TF 681230)

Parking: Roydon Common car park (near PE32 1AS)*

Dog friendly: Yes, but be aware of animals and nesting birds

Public toilets: None

Nearest food: The Three Horseshoes in the village of Roydon does lovely food and a nice cup of coffee

*Coming from King's Lynn, turn right off the roundabout onto the A148; the car park is 200 metres on the right-hand side

3 ROYDON COMMON

The Route

1. Start your walk at the car park just off the A148, adjacent to the model flying club. Take the marked footpath at the southern end of the car park leading into Roydon Common. Almost immediately you will enter a gorse and heathland landscape, with a clear footpath meandering through. Pass the information board on your left and, just 150 metres further, where the footpath divides, take the left-hand turn.

2. Follow the waymarked trail as it heads up a gentle incline and then dips down and skirts some boggy land and springs. You will see a lone oak tree on the horizon; just opposite this is a large, sandy cutaway in the landscape. It is worth climbing to the top of this for a view across the Common. At the end of the path, go through the gate and turn immediately right. Just a few metres on and you will come to a stile that leads out onto further heathland. To your left you will see a tall, disused tower; this was an observation post during the Second World War.

3. The trail, which is about two-thirds of a mile long, takes you along the top of a gentle ridge. Keep the fence to your right and follow the trail to the very end of the ridge, ignoring the two waymarked paths turning down the slope. At the end of the trail, turn left down the slope, past the wild horse corral, and then go through the gate to your right.

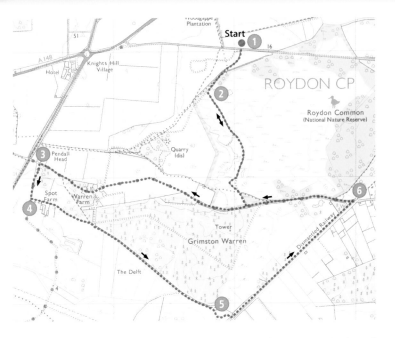

4. Turn immediately left and follow the path as it heads along a grassy track, past wetlands on either side. Watch out for a variety of wildlife here, particularly wildfowl. This area is called the Delft, a word which originates from the Dutch language, meaning canal or waterway.

5. Where Grimston Common ends, you will come to a grassy clearing. Turn left along a farm track and after just a few metres you will see a slightly overgrown path that takes you through the tree line. This is the course of the old railway that used to link London to Hunstanton, passing through the royal residence at Sandringham. For easier walking, you can take the road that runs parallel; both will end at the same spot. This track skirts the edge of Grimston Common and you are likely to see the wild horses grazing along this part of the Common.

6. At the end of the trail, go over the stile and take the left-hand turn past the white cottage (Railway Cottage). You will see the pump in the cottage garden, part of an 18th-century well that draws water from the natural springs in the area. Follow the sandy track through the tree line to the point where it emerges between Grimston Common on your left and Roydon Common on your right. Continue along the path and eventually you will return to the gate by the lone oak tree. Turn right here and retrace your steps back to the car park.

4 SHOULDHAM WOODS

A WALK THROUGH PINE FORESTS AND HEATHLAND.

Shouldham is a thriving Breckland village with an energetic buzz to it. Located on the edge of the woods and heathland of Shouldham Warren but not far from the A10 road to Cambridge and the main rail line to King's Cross, the village is attracting a growing number of people seeking the rural life, while maintaining a busy job in the city.

At the heart of Shouldham is the village green, where the annual beer and music festival takes place over a noisy and fun-packed three days in September. For the remainder of the year, much of the activity centres around the community-owned village pub, the King's Arms – the first of its kind in the county – and the Chalk and Cheese cafe/deli. Both of these establishments offer all-day refreshments, and are geared up for walkers and cyclists.

The village itself is centred around the green with the majority of the houses dating back to Victorian and Edwardian times. Sitting back from the green is the church of All Saints, which dates back to the 15th century, but was rebuilt in part in 1870. There is also the remains of a Gilbertine Abbey just to the north of the village, the site of Abbey Farm today.

Shouldham Warren is a fascinating environment where the sandy heathland of the Brecks and the dark, heavy soils of the Fens merge and the landscape changes quite dramatically. These days the Warren is covered with conifers, ferns and rhododendrons, but from the 17th to 19th centuries it was open heathland and a place where rabbits were bred, nurtured, protected and then trapped for meat and fur. The fur was taken to the nearby towns of Brandon and Thetford where it was made into hats and exported.

During the Second World War, the Warren was used by the armed forces for training purposes and evidence of this can be seen to the east of the car park, where the old rifle butt, ruined buildings and earthworks are thought to be the remains of a camp and shooting range.

The walk starts in the village of Shouldham and for the first mile the route follows a quiet country road. Once you enter the Warren you will be walking on a mix of sandy or loamy paths, pine forest floors and grassy river paths. In the winter, some of the river paths may be boggy, but this is a relatively easy walk, with only the slightest of inclines. While our walk takes in part of the Warren, there are numerous footpaths through the Warren that keen walkers, runners and cyclists can enjoy. This particular walk also gives you some fine views across open farmland as well as the chance to see some bird and wildlife in the foliage alongside the man-made irrigation ditches. Dogs may be off the lead for the majority of this walk.

THE BASICS

Distance: 6 miles / 9.5km

Gradient: Some undulations in the ground but only gentle inclines

Severity: Quite easy

Approx. time to walk: 2½ hours

Stiles: None

Map: OS Explorer 236 (King's Lynn, Downham Market & Swaffham)

Path description: Tarmac road, marked trails and footpaths

Start point: The King's Arms public house (GR TF 676088)

Parking: Roadside parking and at the pub, if you plan to eat there later (PE33 0BY)

Dog friendly: Yes

Public toilets: At the King's Arms at the start of walk

Nearest food: The King's Arms serves food from 12 to 2pm and from 6pm. There is a cafe next door which serves teas, coffees and cakes

4 SHOULDHAM WOODS

The Route

1. The walk starts from the King's Arms car park. Walk from the front of the pub straight across the end of the village green and take the small footpath that runs alongside Tory Cottage. This footpath winds past the school and some paddocks. Ignore the left-hand turn with the footpath sign and instead continue until the path meets New Road. Turn left and follow New Road until it becomes Warren Road. You will pass a playing field on your left. Where the road bends to the right, continue straight on, heading towards the Warren.

2. Follow the tarmac road for approximately 300 metres then turn right onto a woodland path. There is a small car park, with room for about four cars. If you wished to shorten the walk, this would be a good alternative starting point.

3. Follow the woodland path for approximately 200 metres. The Warren is criss-crossed with man-made paths. Take the third turning on your left to follow a narrower grassy track through the trees and bushes. You will come to a crossing point over the deep ditch. Turn left and follow the path that runs between the ditch and the woods. You will see a white farmhouse – Mere Plot Farm – across the ditch. A path goes over the ditch to the farmhouse, but you cross the path and continue straight on.

4. Follow the line of the ditch round to the left and eventually you will see a red-tipped post adjacent to a narrow path that turns left back into the woods. Follow this path through the young trees. At the first opportunity turn right, following the sandy path down a slight incline. Carry straight on at the first crossroads, then take a right turn at a red-tipped marker post. You will come to another ditch; here you turn left and follow the river bank. The fields to your right and the woods to your left are a haven for wildlife, so don't be surprised to see herons, stoats, hares, owls and even the odd glimpse of a kingfisher.

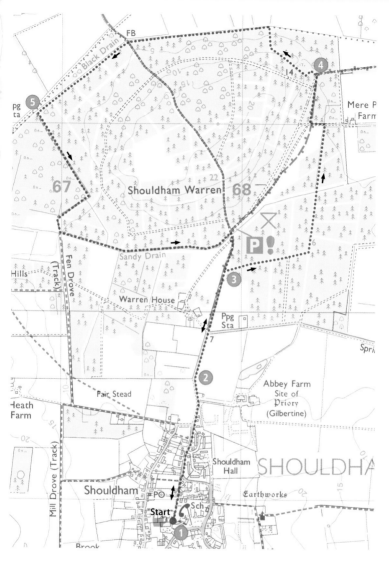

5. You continue to follow the line of the river, past a wooden and iron bridge (pic 5) and a pumping station, until you reach a sharp turn. As the ditch travels to the right, so you turn left and follow the path in a straight line. There are paths off to the left back into the woods, but stick to this path until you come to a larger car park. Turn right and you are now back on Warren Road. Follow this road back to the village. As you come to the place where Warren Road becomes New Road, turn right and follow the road round until it brings you to the front of the King's Arms.

5 GREAT MASSINGHAM

This walk is a gentle five-mile stroll through a typical west Norfolk village and the surrounding countryside. Part of the walk takes in the Peddars Way – a 46-mile-long Roman Road that was used to transport livestock from the west to the east of the county.

Pretty as a picture postcard, the carrstone and flint houses of Great Massingham sit around the village green and the two large duck ponds – there are more, smaller ponds on the outskirts of the village. The ponds were originally fish ponds for the local 11th-century Augustinian Abbey.

Quintessentially an English country village, Great Massingham has a lively and popular pub, the Dabbling Duck, which serves great food and local beers. It also has a church as well as a post office and village shop, which sells a range of foods and drinks to refresh a thirsty walker.

Unusually for a village deep in the rural countryside, Great Massingham is home to a radio transmitting station, broadcasting both KL.FM (King's Lynn Radio) and Radio Norfolk, as well as several digital radio services. A country clothing and agricultural supply shop also sits on the outskirts of the village and, if you are looking to stock up on wellington boots, socks or walking clothes, it is worth a peek.

Great Massingham played an important role during the Second World War when it was a satellite RAF base, supporting the main station at RAF West Raynham. While the airfield has been returned to farmland, the runways and some evidence of its wartime exploits remain visible.

Three guest rooms in the Dabbling Duck are named after pilots who were stationed in the village who went on to become household names in sport. Probably the most famous of these pilots was Kenneth Wolstenholme – he went on to become a football commentator and achieved legendary status when he uttered the words 'They think it's all over… It is now.' The other two pilots were Keith Miller, the Australian cricketer and Bill Edrich, the fastest England bowler of his generation. Perhaps not unsurprisingly, the squadron played cricket to relax between missions.

It is thought that the village dates back to the fifth century, when the village was inhabited by a group of Angles and Saxons, who moved in after the Romans departed. The group's leader was called Maesron, and the community were known as Maersings, hence the name

'Massingham'. The centre of the village is dominated by the great square tower of the 15th-century St Mary's Church. Like so many of the beautiful churches in Norfolk, St Mary's has a well-proportioned structure with diagonal buttresses tapering up in four stages to the battlements and corner pinnacles. It has four bells, which were last re-cast in 1903.

Among the Great Massingham alumni is Britain's first Prime Minister, Sir Robert Walpole. He was educated in Great Massingham and later in life built the breathtakingly beautiful Houghton Hall, just five miles away.

THE BASICS

Distance: 5 miles / 8km
Gradient: Flat
Severity: Quite easy
Approx. time to walk: 2½ hours
Stiles: None
Map: OS Explorer 250 (Norfolk Coast West)
Path description: Road, marked trails, fields and footpaths
Start point: Village green, Great Massingham (GR TF 797229)
Parking: The village green, free parking (PE32 2HN)
Dog friendly: Yes, but be aware of animals and nesting birds
Public toilets: The Dabbling Duck Public House
Nearest food: The Dabbling Duck serves food and drink and the Post Office has a good range of baked goods as well as snacks and drinks

5 GREAT MASSINGHAM

The Route

1. Starting from the Dabbling Duck, turn right, keeping the village sign and duck pond on your left. Cross over Lynn Lane and continue down Castleacre Road. Turn right into Drunken Drove, past the fields of cattle and follow it until you come to the Peddars Way on your right (opposite a road on your left).

2. Take the Peddars Way (one of the best known Roman Roads in the area) and follow it until you come to a large stone with a poem etched on it (You will have passed several footpaths on your right, which all lead back into the village). Take the bridleway on the right just after the stone.

3. Follow this path until you come to a T-junction, where you bear right, keeping Nutwood on your right. Follow th track until you reach a farm yard, walk through the yard to a road. At the road (church Lane) turn right and walk about 150 mts until you reach a footpath on your left.

4. Follow the path for approx. 170 mts, you will then reach Mad Dog Lane. Turn left and follow this lane for ¾ mile (it will merge with Walcup's Lane). When you reach a junction that joins Walcup's Lane, go right and take the footpath that passes the pond and joins Abbey Road and leads you back to the start point and the Dabbling Duck.

One of several stones along the route of the Peddars Way which are part of "A Norfolk Songline", a multimedia arts project inspired by the Peddars Way. This stone is inscribed with:

From Blackwater Carr to Seagate
Since the plough first broke the bread of land
Pightles and pieces plots & pastur

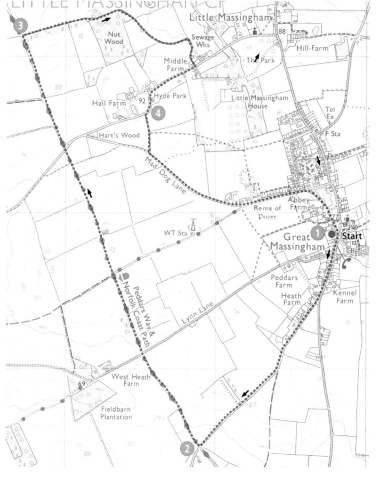

6 CASTLE ACRE

THIS SIX-MILE WALK STARTS AND ENDS IN THE POPULAR AND THRIVING VILLAGE OF CASTLE ACRE, WITH ITS PUB, THE OSTRICH, TEA ROOM AND COFFEE SHOP/CAFE. THE HEART OF THE VILLAGE IS THE VILLAGE GREEN, BUT CASTLE ACRE'S SIGNIFICANCE IN EARLIER TIMES IS EVIDENCED BY THE RUINS OF THE CASTLE AND PRIORY THAT LAY AT EITHER END OF THE VILLAGE.

The walk also takes in the hamlet of South Acre and skirts along the pretty village of West Acre – a small, hamlet community that punches above its weight with a garden centre, a pub and a thriving theatre.

Throughout the walk you will have cause to stop and take a closer look. The castle walls that lie to the east of the green are all but gone, but the arched gateway into the village remains. The castle itself is in ruins but some careful preservation and well-designed information boards help you piece together an idea of how the village looked in medieval times.

Both the castle and the priory were founded soon after the Norman Conquest of 1066. During its heyday, Castle Acre play an important role in the affairs of state and when it was first established the village was one of the finest examples of town planning during the Norman period. It was a fortified town and its magnificence reflected the importance of this part of East Anglia, largely due to the region's wealthy wool and grain trade at this time.

The castle was of motte and bailey construction and was strategically built where the ancient trackway of the Peddars Way crossed the River Nar. This location was vital for both fortification and riverborne trade.

The priory was built and then rebuilt. Its first site was within the walls of the castle, but this was deemed too small and a year later, in 1089, it was relocated. It was founded by William de Warenne, who also founded England's first ever Cluniac priory in Lewes in Sussex.

The walk takes in both the castle and the priory, but once out of the village you will experience a whole raft of Norfolk countryside, from the boggy marshes to the south of the castle to the sandy breckland as you cross the expansive farmland. The woods and plantations are alive with wildlife: expect to see rabbits, hares and many varieties of deer – the native red deer, fallow deer and roebuck as well as the Chinese import, muntjac.

The woody areas – with a natural range of native tree species – are also home to large toadstools, bluebells and primroses and the hedgerows are varied with blackthorn, dog rose and brambles. Around the low-lying area surrounding the priory, watch out for barn owls and tawny owls, and if you are in the area at sunset make sure you have your camera ready for some stunning colours as the sun plays on the reeds and old brick walls.

THE BASICS

Distance: 6½ miles / 10.2km

Gradient: Some slight inclines

Severity: Quite easy

Approx. time to walk: 3 hours

Stiles: None

Map: OS Explorer 236 (King's Lynn, Downham Market & Swaffham)

Path description: Quiet roads, marked trails, fields and footpaths; the walk from the castle can be boggy in winter and spring

Start point: The village green, Castle Acre (GR TF 816151)

Parking: The village green, free parking (PE32 2AE)

Dog friendly: Yes, but be aware of animals and nesting birds

Public toilets: The Ostrich pub

Nearest food: The Ostrich or the Castle Acre Tea Rooms – both adjacent to the Village Green

6 CASTLE ACRE

The Route

1. The walk starts at the village green. You can park along the side of the green, in front of the Ostrich pub or the tea room. Head east along High Street towards the ruins of the castle wall. Turn right into Pyes Lane, and this will take you to the ruined castle itself – this Norman castle is worth taking a few minutes to explore.

2. Leave the grounds of the castle by the southerly corner and follow the footpath that takes you across the marsh. (Be aware that this can get quite boggy in wet weather.) You will emerge onto the Sporle/Little Dunham road, and will come to a fork in the road. Stay left and continue straight on until your road joins with Southacre Road. Turn left and follow the road. After approximately 500 metres you will come to a ford. The footpath skirts this ford and you continue to follow the road. After about two-thirds of a mile you will pass Church Farm on your left. Shortly after, you will come to a triangle in the road; keep to the right and follow the road round, passing The Rectory on your right and South Acre Hall on your left.

3. About 300 metres past South Acre Hall, you will see a footpath on the left-hand side. Follow this as it passes across fields and through Fingerhill Plantation. You will pass a small reservoir on your right and, shortly after, the track comes to a crossroads. Turn right and follow the tree-lined track. This track continues for about one mile. You will cross another track before passing a triangle-shaped plantation on your right. Just before you reach a tarmac road, turn right along another path. This takes you across fields and through two plantations.

4. Where the track meets the Narford road, continue straight across. You will see chapel ruins in the field to your right as you cross the road. Continue along the path until you come to a crossroads. This is the edge of the village of West Acre. The trail continues from the crossroads where the two tracks meet. Follow the marked path that turns sharply right. You will come to a footbridge over a ford. Once over the water, turn left and then swing to the right onto a clear track. This track, Mill Lane, follows the course of the River Nar and crosses Castle Acre Common. Eventually you will come to Common Road; follow this to the first right-hand turn. This is Priory Road and a short detour will take you into the grounds of the Abbey itself. This is a National Trust property and worth a visit.

5. Returning to Priory Road, follow this road back to the village, entering the heart of the village from the opposite end. Follow the road until you see Bailey Street on the right-hand side, turn here and you will be back at the Green.

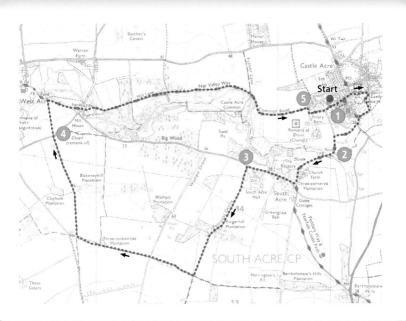

7 PINGOS AND BRECKLAND

WHAT IS A PINGO? THEY WERE ORIGINALLY LOW HILLOCKS THAT FORMED IN PERMAFROST (TUNDRA) CONDITIONS 20,000 YEARS AGO DURING THE LAST ICE AGE. THESE PREHISTORIC FEATURES WERE FORMED WHEN WATER BENEATH THE SURFACE FROZE TO FORM LENSES OF ICE PUSHING SOIL UPWARDS, FORMING A SMALL HILLOCK. DURING THE SUMMER THAW, THE SOIL ON THE SURFACE WOULD SLUDGE OFF AND ACCUMULATE AROUND THE PERIPHERY OF THE HILLOCKS. SHALLOW CRATERS WERE LEFT WHEN THE ICE FINALLY MELTED, CAUSING THE HILLOCKS TO COLLAPSE.

At the start and end of this fascinating walk, you will see many examples of pingos, small, water-filled depressions in the ground, usually filled with water. They make an ideal habitat and breeding area for a number of native species.

You will also pass Thompson Water, a large reservoir of 40 acres, created in 1845 by the draining of a tributary of the River Wissey. Thompson Water is owned and managed by Norfolk Wildlife Trust, the oldest wildlife trust in England.

This whole area is alive with wildlife and native British plants and trees. Yellow water lilies are abundant on the open water, as well as wintering wildfowl. Thompson Carr is damp woodland with alder and oak and you may be lucky enough to spot an elusive roe deer through the trees.

There are many small natural ponds on Thompson Common, which is also the best location in the country to see the scarce emerald damselfly, among other more common species. Thompson Common is lowland grassland, which is enhanced by the open water and fen communities of the pingos. Parts of Thompson Common are grazed by a herd of Shetland ponies.

The village of Thompson is one of the Breckland villages. The Brecks area is on the Norfolk/Suffolk border and is one of the most distinctive landscapes in the UK. Apart from anything else, it boasts its best overall climate with low rainfall and hot summers.

The feeling that this is an ancient landscape is also enhanced by the vegetation that grows. There are heathlands that were created in prehistoric times by the tribes that settled in the area, felling and burning the native forests. Interspersed among these are rows of Scots Pines, called 'deal rows' locally. Many of these are maintained as natural hedge lines, but the fact they are not native is given away by the linearity of the growth.

As you follow this walk, you really will feel as if you have stepped back in history.

THE BASICS

Distance: 6 miles / 9.5km

Gradient: Nearly all flat

Severity: Quite easy

Approx. time to walk: 2½ hours

Stiles: None

Map: OS Explorer 229 (Thetford Forest in the Brecks)

Path description: Marked trails and footpaths, one slightly boggy part by the river

Start point: Great Eastern Pingo Trail car park, Stow Bedon (GR TL 940966)

Parking: Car park just behind lay-by at the former Stow Bedon railway station, off A1075 (NR17 1DP)

Dog friendly: Yes, but be aware of animals and nesting birds

Public toilets: None

Nearest food: The Three Chequers in the village of Thompson (slight diversion of 300 metres to get there)

7 PINGOS AND BRECKLAND

The Route

1. Starting at the free car park, ignore the disused railway track straight in front of you and instead take the gate on the right which takes you onto Thompson Common.

2. A waymarked path takes you across wetlands and through woodlands. Almost immediately you will start to see small pingos, for which this walk is named. Follow the winding trail over this piece of land. The pathway is varied as deer and sheep tracks mix with human tracks to criss-cross the common. You are heading west and after around three-quarters of a mile you will meet a surfaced lane.

3. Turn left and follow the lane. You will pass a few isolated buildings – houses and farm buildings – and eventually the lane finishes and an unsurfaced track takes over. As the track bears right, so you need to go left, crossing an extensive area of grassland. Keep your dog on a lead here as sheep may be grazing. The trail across the grassland is marked with waymarkers.

4. The route takes you through Thompson Carr, following the edge of a stream through quite dense woodland. At the end of the stream, turn right, cross the stream and walk to the next junction (approx.. 200 metres).

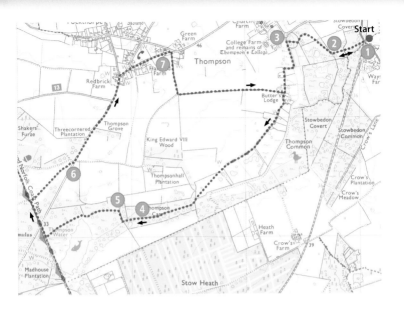

5. Turn left and follow the path, past Thompson Water on your left. This area is managed by the Norfolk Naturalists' Trust. Just past this point, you will meet the Peddars Way – the ancient drovers' track that links east and west Norfolk. Follow the Peddars Way for approximately 300 metres before turning right. This is also the edge of a military firing ground, so do not venture over the wire fence!

6. Turn right down a long, straight tarmac road. This is open to traffic but is very quiet. The road takes you right into the village of Thompson. Pass the first turning on your left and at the crossroads you can either carry straight on to the Chequers Public House or you can take the right-hand turn which takes you past the village school.

7. Just past the school, cross the road and follow Hall Lane. This is marked with a bridleway sign. A track crosses agricultural land. At the junction, turn left, following a well-used farm track. Cross a field following the footpath and then join a tarmac-surfaced road. Turn left along a quiet road and after a third of a mile you will see a turning back into the woods. Here you cross the common land and retrace your steps to return to the car park.

8 OXBOROUGH HALL

A short walk with a long history.

This short, easy walk is a meander around the village of Oxborough and the surrounding farmlands. While the walk is not as challenging as many others in this book, it is nonetheless a delightful amble, taking in the sights and sounds of the countryside.

The village of Oxborough, lying on the eastern edge of the Norfolk Brecklands, is dominated by its grand medieval moated country house, Oxburgh Hall, which was built in 1482 by Sir Edmund Bedingfeld. Since then it has been altered and built upon, each new construction depicting a different era – a fortified gatehouse built in 1772, Flemish-syle stepped gables built in Victorian times and terracotta chimneys added at the start of the Edwardian period.

Just recently, Oxburgh has gone through another transformation, with an army of volunteers and specialists working together on a conservation project that has revealed more of the Hall's past splendours. Among these are more than 130 different samples of wallpapers that had been stored in the attic. Some of these date back to the late 1700s.

One of the most famous guests at Oxburgh Hall, albeit not a voluntary house guest, was Mary, Queen of Scots. She was imprisoned in England, in the custody of the Earl of Shrewsbury, and during a stay at Oxburgh Hall the exiled Queen worked on a tapestry, known as at the Oxburgh Hangings.

The Hall has made several television appearances, most notably in Dad's Army, You Rang, M'Lord, and the 1994 film, Love on a Branch Line. It is now in the care of the National Trust.

The village itself covers just five square miles and has a population of roughly 250 people. The surrounding area is a typical Breckland mix of farmland, woodland and heath – a unique landscape of great historical and ecological interest. The roads are lined with gnarled and twisted pine trees, which look spectacular against the backdrop of a setting sun. And the area is home to a vast array of wildlife: more than 12,845 different species inhabit the Brecks, some of which are found nowhere else in the UK.

While we are all familiar with the brazen muntjac and the swooping flocks of swifts, this area is also home to many more, lesser-known, shy creatures. Among some of the wildlife and plant life that can be seen in the area are white admiral and yellow brimstone butterflies, otters, voles, red and roe deer, nightjars, firecrest adders and the elusive but beautiful golden pheasant.

Depending upon the time of year you visit, you may also find yourself walking in or beside a carpet of purple heather, while the margins of fields are often ablaze with colourful flowers such as viper's bugloss.

THE BASICS

Distance: 3½ miles / 5.5km

Gradient: Fairly level

Severity: Easy

Approx time to walk: 1¾ hours

Stiles: Three

Map: OS Explorer 236 (King's Lynn, Downham Market & Swaffham)

Path description: Paths, footpaths and country lanes

Start point: Bedingfeld Arms public house, opposite Oxburgh Hall (GR TF 743013)

Parking: Roadside parking or the pub if you plan to eat there (PE33 9PS)

Dog friendly: Can run free, but must be under control on farmland and able to manage the stiles

Public toilets: None on route

Nearest food: The Bedingfeld Arms

The Route

1. From the Bedingfeld Arms car park turn right. You will catch a glimpse of Oxburgh Hall (pic 1a) through the trees just to your left, and this beautiful old manor house is worth a visit if you have time. Follow the road to the cross roads, passing the old ruined church on your left-hand side.

2. Cross over the road onto Eastmoor Road. Although this is a very quiet road, do watch out for traffic. After approximately 650 metres, take the footpath across the farmland to your right. The signed path may be partially obscured by crops, but take a diagonal direction north until you reach the end of the second field. Turn left and follow the grassy field-edge track as it runs alongside the wooded area. The grassy field-edge track runs into a sandy farm track with a line of trees on either side. Follow this and eventually you reach a lane by a barn. Turn right here onto a tarmac road. You will just be able to distinguish the earthworks of old St Mary's Church in the field to your left.

3. Following the tarmac road, after about 550 metres, the lane bends sharp right towards Gooderstone and Oxborough. Follow this straight road to a junction. Go straight across, down the road marked 'Unsuitable for HGVs'.

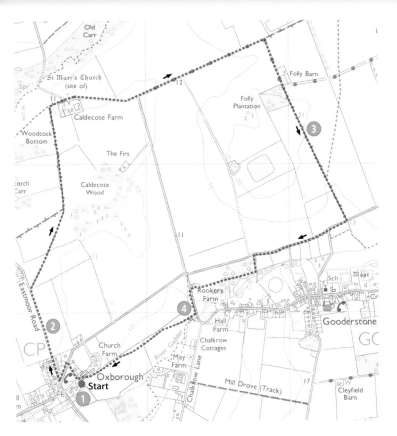

4. Look for the footpath sign on your right, which will be before the bridge over the River Gadder, and immediately adjacent to the Anglian Water works. Cross a stile, and walk straight across the meadow ahead, heading for the gate in the distance. When you reach it, continue in the same direction until you reach another stile in the far corner of the field. Turn left and head for the row

of tall trees until you reach a third stile by a house. Turn left and then follow the pathway as it winds behind the houses. You will eventually emerge onto a path with the village green ahead. Walk to the end of the green and the Bedingfeld Arms is on your left.

9 RINGSTEAD

THIS IS A TRADITIONAL NORFOLK COASTAL VILLAGE WITH MANY OF ITS HOUSES MADE FROM LOCAL CARRSTONE AND FLINT, USUALLY WITH A RED PANTILE ROOF. IT IS SURROUNDED ON ALL SIDES BY ROLLING COUNTRYSIDE — MOSTLY AGRICULTURAL LAND, BUT WITH THE ADDED INTEREST OF THE RINGSTEAD DOWNS, A UNIQUE GEOGRAPHICAL FEATURE.

Ringstead itself has a number of houses dating back to the 17th and 18th centuries and the community has grown out of the thriving agricultural economy that developed from the 15th century onwards. Part of the ancient route of the Peddars Way passes through Ringstead, indicating that it was one of the villages on the route from the south to the east of the county that was so popular with drovers and tradesmen. While the Peddars Way itself is a 46-mile route from Thetford to Holme-next-the-Sea, it is believed the route is part of a much longer pathway running from Lyme Regis in Dorset to Hunstanton, thus linking the south and east coasts. Recent archaeological evidence has suggested the Peddars Way pre-dates Roman times.

Today the village is relatively well served for a small rural community. It has a well-stocked village shop that sells everything from everyday provisions through to specialist magazines, biodynamic wine and a huge array of wild bird foods. The Gin Trap public house, which dates back to the 17th century, serves good food and has managed to retain a local, community feel as well as catering for the large tourist footfall. The village hall regularly hosts art exhibitions and there is a garden nursery, Wards, which is well known throughout the county for its high-quality plants and seeds.

Ringstead Downs is one of the largest remaining areas of chalk grassland in the county, and this attractive, steep-sided valley supports a diverse range of plant and animal species. Many interesting plants can be found, as well as around twenty species of butterfly. Several nationally declining birds – yellowhammer, whitethroat and linnet – occur in good numbers.

If you walk on the Downs from June to September, you will see a proliferation of lemon-yellow flowers. This is the Common Rock Rose, a strongly scented creeping perennial that is typically found on chalky grassland.

THE BASICS

Distance: 6 miles / 9.5km (7 miles / 11.25km if you choose the beach route)

Gradient: Some slight inclines

Severity: Quite easy

Approx. time to walk: 3½ hours

Stiles: None

Map: OS Explorer 250 (Norfolk Coast West)

Path description: Quiet roads, marked trails, fields and footpaths. One section on the beach as an option

Start point: The Gin Trap Inn, Ringstead (GR TF 706403)

Parking: Considerate roadside parking or the pub if you plan to eat there (PE36 5JU)

Dog friendly: Yes

Public toilets: At Holme-next-the-Sea and Hunstanton

Nearest food: At Ringstead, the Gin Trap for meals and the General Stores village shop sells snacks. At Hunstanton the Beach Cafe serves teas, coffees and light meals.

9 RINGSTEAD

The Route

1. Leave the Gin Trap Inn and turn right past the General Stores. Follow the road up a slight incline past the church on your right and a number of houses, built from the traditional Norfolk carrstone and flint. As you reach the corner, ignore the turning towards Hunstanton and carry on around the right-hand bend.

2. Follow this road as it swings to the left. You will see a disused windmill in the fields to your left. Continue along the road, past the row of houses and the solitary large house on the brow of the hill. As you walk past the paddock, you will see a footpath to your right. Take this and after approximately 150 metres turn left, down a slight incline.

3. This path takes you directly down to the village of Holme-next-the-Sea. Cross the A149 and continue straight ahead. Follow this road all the way through the village, past the White Horse pub, until you reach the T-junction.

4. Turn right along Beach Road and once you cross the small hump-backed bridge look for the waymarked path that runs behind the caravan park. You are now following a footpath that runs alongside the River Hun. Follow this path until it emerges onto the road that leads into Hunstanton Golf Club.

5. Cross the golf course to join the footpath that runs through the dunes. This is part of the Norfolk Coastal Path. You can now choose to walk either on the beach or through the dunes. Follow the route towards Hunstanton, past the lifeboat station; you will eventually see the iconic red and white cliffs in the distance. For refreshments, the Beach Cafe is 50 metres off the beach next door to the lifeboat station.

6. When you reach the foot of the cliffs, turn left up the steps to the clifftop car park. Walk across the car park towards the lighthouse. When you reach the lighthouse, turn left and follow the road to the A149.

7. Cross the A149 into Chapel Bank. Follow the lane to the corner and then turn right to follow the waymarked footpath (known as Lover's Lane). Follow this path and when you reach the solitary house, continue to follow the path as it diverts around the house and garden.

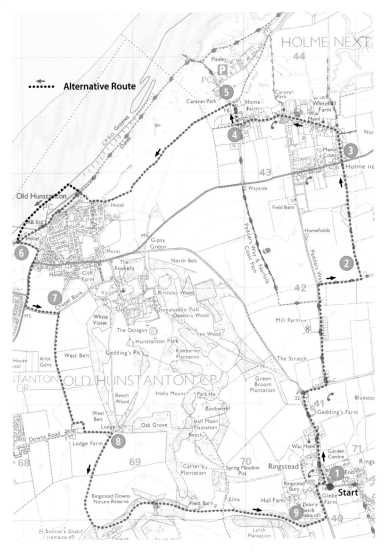

8. At the country lane turn left and follow the road for approximately 200 metres before it again becomes a track. This takes you down to a house and farm. Turn left and follow the path through the farmyard. You will pass through a kissing gate and enter the Ringstead Downs.

9. Follow the footpath through the Ringstead Downs and at the end of the grassy track pass through the gate towards the road. Cross the road and turn left, following the field edge. As you pass a large house on your left, follow the road as it bends to the right. Follow this around, past the Village Hall and you will see the Gin Trap ahead.

10 HOLKHAM TO WELLS-NEXT-THE-SEA

Holkham Hall has been the family seat of the Coke family and the Earls of Leicester since it was built between 1734 and 1764 by Thomas Coke, the first Earl of Leicester. The Coke family has actually lived in the village for much longer – Sir Edward Coke, who founded the family fortune, bought an Elizabethan Manor House (Hill Hall) in 1609.

It was Thomas Coke who, inspired by his six-year tour of Europe, came up with the plans for Holkham Hall. He wanted a Palladian-style mansion which reflected some of the classical buildings he had seen on his tour of Europe's great cities.

To turn his vision to reality, Thomas employed the architect Matthew Brettingham to oversee the work of interpreting and implementing the designs for the new house drawn up by the architect William Kent and himself.

Work on the new home began in 1734 but it was thirty years before it was completed. The great brain behind it, Thomas, died before his dream became reality and so his widow, Lady Margaret Tufton, took on the project and the house was completed.

It was Thomas Coke's great-nephew – also Thomas Coke – who perhaps brought the greatest level of fame to Holkham. Known as Coke of Norfolk, he introduced a number of innovations to agriculture, including selective breeding – to get the best livestock – and crop rotation, which helped soil quality. It was this work that caused people to credit Thomas Coke with the start of the Agricultural Revolution – a movement that put Norfolk on the map as a great agricultural economy.

The house and grounds at Holkham Hall, which you will see from many angles on this walk, are little changed from the first Earl of Leicester's plans. The house is a classic example of Palladian architecture based on the ancient temples of Greece and Rome. The emphasis is on symmetry and great views in all directions – as Holkham Hall sits proudly at the heart of the estate, you can see what Thomas Coke was aiming for.

The Holkham estate is vast, covering some 6,000 hectares. While the majority is given over to agriculture, some land is set aside for conservation, game and agri-environment projects. The estate has 22 tenant farmers, besides its own in-house farming company. It also owns 300 homes in Holkham, Wells and the surrounding villages and has a number of diverse businesses in its portfolio, including the Beach Cafe next to Wells Beach.

The walk takes in part of the grounds of Holkham Hall, meanders into the coastal town of Wells and returns via the strikingly beautiful Holkham Beach.

© Holkham Estate

THE BASICS

Distance: 6 miles / 9.5km

Gradient: Mostly flat with one steep set of steps to the beach

Severity: Medium – the beach can make walking difficult

Approx. time to walk: 3 hours

Stiles: None

Map: OS Explorer 251 (Norfolk Coast Central)

Path description: Minor road, grassy tracks, sandy beach

Start point: The Victoria Inn, Holkham (GR TF 892438)

Parking: The Victoria Inn car park (NR23 1RG)

Dog friendly: Dogs should be kept on leads in the deer park*

Public toilets: Opposite the Victoria Hotel, in the town centre at Wells and at the Beach Cafe

Refreshments: A choice of cafes and restaurants in Wells town centre and the Beach Cafe at Wells Beach

*(Quick tip: Deer are notorious for carrying ticks, so make sure your dog's tick and flea treatment is up to date)

The Route

1. Our walk starts in the car park of the Victoria Hotel in the village of Holkham at the end of the drive up to Holkham House. From here you turn right and follow the tarmac drive up to the gates of Holkham Hall. Turn left once you have passed through the formal gateway and follow a broad track through the woodland and deer park. There is every chance that deer will be roaming here, so keep dogs on a lead.

2. Go through the gate and continue until you come to a junction of five tracks. Take the first track on the left, a surfaced path leading through Mousehill Plantation to East Lodge. Here the track meets the road, a sharp bend in the A149. Follow the pavement past the community hospital and continue towards the town itself.

3. Where the A149 turns right, follow the road straight ahead into the town. You will pass a Congregational church and public conveniences on your left. To your right is Buttlands and just a few metres further you will see Staithe Street on your left. Turn down here and follow the street to the quayside. Our route takes us left along the quay, but it is worth spending a little time exploring the quay area with its working fishermen's boats and pretty coastal cottages.

4. Turn left and follow the quay past the large Dutch boat which sells pancakes and beers – and at the end of the quay turn right. This takes you past the Harbourmaster's office. You now follow the raised embankment all the way to the beach. To your right you will spot a small island. This is East Hills, a stretch of beach and pine trees that can only be reached by boat or at low tide.

5. At the end of the embankment you will find the lifeboat station and the Wells Beach Cafe. This is a good place to stop for refreshments. Head towards the pine forests to the left of the cafe. You will soon encounter a set of steps that takes you through the pine woods and onto the beach. You descend onto the beach through the row of brightly coloured beach huts.

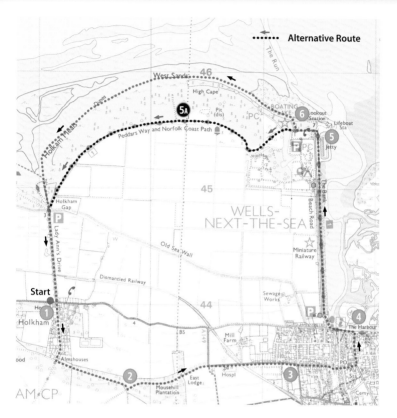

5A. As an alternative to the beach, you can choose to walk through the pine forests. From the Beach Cafe, walk past the steps to the beach and instead follow the path that runs to the right of the woodlands. Go past the boating lake and through the gate. After approximately 100

metres, you will come to a waymarked fork. Go left here and then turn right at a T-junction to continue along a track by the edge of the wood. This track also emerges at the Holkham Gap. Turn left and you are on Lady Anne's Drive and it is a straightforward walk back to the Victoria.

6. Follow the beach westwards until you come to Holkham Gap – a break in the woods. Follow the boardwalk through the trees until you emerge onto Lady Ann Drive. This takes you back to the A149 and just over the road is the Victoria Hotel.

CREAKE ABBEY BEGAN LIFE AS ST MARY'S ABBEY, ORIGINALLY A HOSPITAL IN THE 12TH CENTURY. IT WAS DISSOLVED IN 1506 AFTER ALL THE MONKS DIED OF THE PLAGUE, BUT ITS RUINS REMAIN THE CENTREPIECE FOR THE START OF OUR WALK.

Creake Abbey is now home to a thriving monthly farmers' market (the first Saturday of every month) as well as permanent shops and an award-winning cafe, which is open from 8am until 5pm throughout the year.

The walk will take in the outlying boundary of Holkham Hall, home to the Coke family since 1764, when the first Earl of Leicester, Thomas Coke, commissioned the architects Lord Burlington and William Kent to build a Palladian-style stately home. These days, the Hall remains the home of the Coke family, but is also a thriving tourist attraction, with shop, cafe, tours of the house and gardens and numerous events throughout the year. The village of Holkham is home to the renowned Victoria Hotel, which serves food and drink throughout the day, as well as Holkham Beach, regularly voted one of the best beaches in the UK.

This walk also takes in the lovely little village of Burnham Thorpe, birthplace of Admiral Lord Nelson, the seafaring hero who led England to a famous and decisive victory in the series of Napoleonic Wars at the Battle of Trafalgar in 1805.

Indeed, the great naval hero pops up at regular intervals on this walk. You will tread the footpath Nelson is thought to have walked when he visited the Earl of Leicester at Holkham Hall to get a signature enabling him to draw his pay from the Admiralty; you will see the church where Nelson's father was rector and where his parents are buried; and you will pass the place where Nelson was born. That building has gone, demolished in 1803, but a plaque on the wall of the parsonage marks the spot.

Aside from the historical sites along the way, this six-mile walk also passes through lovely rolling countryside, where hedgerows and coppices encourage a thriving wildlife population. Watch out for hares, red deer, fallow deer, buzzards and hawks, owls at twilight and the occasional kite with its distinctively shaped tail feathers. The hedgerows also offer up an abundance of blackberries and sloes, and you might spot some activity here from harvest mice and hedgehogs.

On the domestic animal front, Holkham Farm Estate and its neighbours rear hundreds of free-range pigs and sheep, so your travels may be accompanied by a background of baas and oinks.

THE BASICS

Distance: 6 miles / 9.5km

Gradient: Mostly flat, a few gentle slopes

Severity: Quite easy

Approx. time to walk: 2½ hours

Stiles: None

Map: OS Explorer 251 (Norfolk Coast Central)

Path description: Marked trails, field boundaries, tarmac roads and footpaths

Start point: Creake Abbey Cafe car park (GR TF 855393)

Parking: Creake Abbey Cafe car park* (NR21 9LF)

Dog friendly: Yes, but be aware of farm animals in the neighbouring fields

Public toilets: At Creake Abbey

Nearest food: Creake Abbey Cafe

*Park at Creake Abbey on the field designated for parking in front of the cafe and shops

The Route

1. Leave the field via the 'exit' route then turn right towards the Abbey. Go past the Abbey and take the first right-hand track that loops behind the buildings housing the cafe and shops. Follow this path for about half a mile. It runs besides a minor road before it becomes a wide farm track that runs alongside three large fields.

2. After crossing three T-junctions where one farm track crosses another, turn left and follow the track as it turns into a tarmac farm road. You will pass a lovely example of an old Norfolk barn.

3. Where the track meets the minor road, turn right and after approximately 400 metres turn left to follow the footpath that takes you along the boundary of Holkham Hall.

4. After half a mile, you reach a wide farm track on the left-hand side; follow this for about three-quarters of a mile. You will go past a fine flint-and-brick barn on your left-hand side. Eventually the track meets a minor road; cross this and head down towards the church. This is the church where Nelson's parents are buried and where his father was rector.

5. Turn left just before the church entrance and follow the road. Where this road meets another, stay right and follow the road into the village of Burnham Thorpe. There is a village green with the public house, inevitably called The Lord Nelson, on the far side.

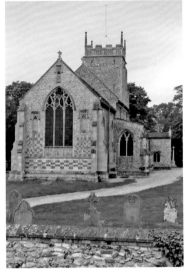

6. Go straight across the junction and then, at the next staggered crossroads, take the road ahead. Follow this past a couple of

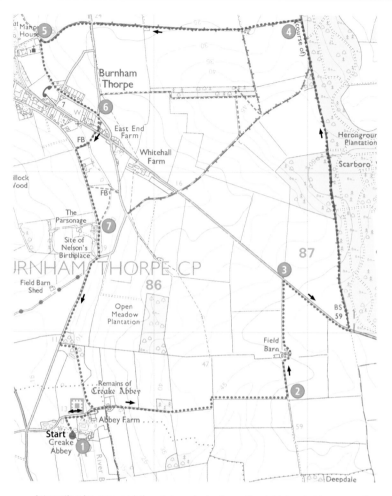

interesting houses, and then take a footpath on the right-hand side across the meadows. This takes you across the River Burn.

7.   Leave the field where the footpath meets the B1355 road and turn left. Sticking to the road, you will pass the building bearing the plaque signifying Nelson's birthplace. Keep on this road, which is a very quiet one, for just over a mile. You will see a footpath marked on the left-hand side, which takes you through a hedge. This takes you into meadowland; follow the clearly defined path across the field. There are sheep here, so dogs must be on a lead. The path takes you back to the Abbey. Pass through a kissing gate and follow the tarmac road to the right. After 300 yards, turn left through the gateway and you will see the car park ahead of you.

12 LITTLE WALSINGHAM

TODAY, THOUSANDS OF PEOPLE VISIT WALSINGHAM EVERY YEAR, MANY ATTENDING THE DAILY MASS AT THE SLIPPER CHAPEL, BUT JUST AS MANY ARE SIMPLY FOLLOWING IN THE FOOTSTEPS OF THE PILGRIMS WHO HAVE VISITED THE VILLAGE SINCE MEDIEVAL TIMES.

In the 14th and 15th century, Walsingham was on a par with Rome when it came to religious importance. Pilgrims came from all over the world to worship at the priory in Little Walsingham.

Why was this small Norfolk hamlet so important? The story dates back to 1061 when Lady Richeldis, who owned Walsingham Manor, had a vision. In this dream she was visited by Mary, mother of Jesus and taken to Nazareth to be shown the house where Jesus was born. In the vision, Mary asked her to build a replica house in Walsingham. This she did – a simple wooden structure housing a statue of Mary with a priory surrounding it.

This shrine in Walsingham remained on the pilgrim route until Henry VIII's Reformation in the 1500s. He ordered this symbol of Catholicism to be destroyed and the statue of Mary was taken to London to be burnt.

In 1897, four hundred years after Henry's rampages, a Roman Catholic pilgrimage to the restored 14th-century Slipper Chapel was the beginning of a new era for Walsingham. The Slipper Chapel is at the centre of the Roman Catholic National Shrine. A replica of Lady Richeldis's shrine was built in 1931 and daily mass is now held for the many visitors that flock here.

The village itself has some lovely old medieval streets containing interesting shops. There is also a museum containing a courthouse from the times of George III. The main attractions, however, are the religious sites and the remains of the priory. A steam railway brings visitors to Little Walsingham from Wells next the Sea on the Wells & Walsingham Light Railway.

THE BASICS

Distance: 5 miles / 8km

Gradient: Easy

Severity: An easy walk

Approx. time to walk: 2½ hours

Stiles: None

Map: OS Explorer 251 (Norfolk Coast Central)

Path description: Minor road, field edges and grassy tracks; some paths are a little overgrown in places

Start point: The Memorial Hall car park, Coker's Hill (GR TF 933369)

Parking: The Memorial Hall car park (NR22 6BN)

Dog friendly: You will pass through farmland so keep dogs under close control

Public toilets: None at start, although toilet facilities are available in the cafes

Nearest food: Tearoom and cafe in the High Street, the Norton Cafe Bar at the Anglican Shrine and Great Walsingham Cafe at Great Walsingham Barns, The Swallows serves meals and snacks all day

The Route

1. Walk along the main street towards Fakenham; you will see the ruined friary on your right. Continue along this road as it leaves the village. You will see a single farm building on the left; go past this and then turn left along an unsurfaced road, which rises into woodland. The lane continues into more open surroundings as you walk up the incline. Once over the hill, the lane continues; when you come to a fork, stay right. Ignore the waymarked permissive path on your right and continue straight ahead. The lane becomes narrower and more enclosed before it emerges onto a road. This is Great Snoring. Turn left and follow the tarmac road into the village.

2. You will cross two junctions before passing Top Farm on your left-hand side. After a further 100 metres turn left down the waymarked permissive path. This route

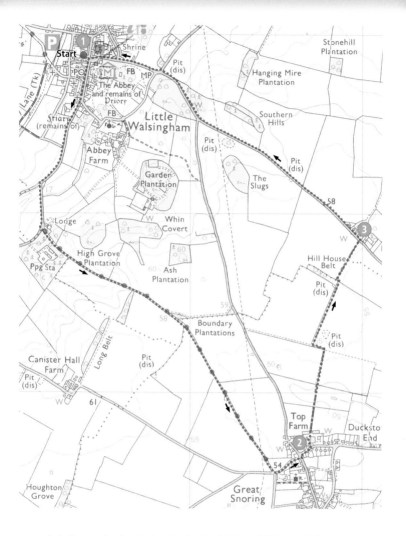

winds through the farm before leaving the buildings behind and following a broad, fenced grassy track. Eventually you will come to a gate and stile, which you pass through. This takes you along the edge of a field. At a junction, turn left and then, just a short walk along, turn right alongside a large field. You are heading to Hill House Farm. At the next boundary go straight ahead, keeping the hedge to your left.

3. At Hill House Farm you will join a minor road. Turn left and follow the road towards Little Walsingham. You will pass a Second World War pillbox as you descend the hill into the village. Bear right, passing the Anglican Shrine before reaching the centre of the village and the car park.

13 CLEY NEXT THE SEA

CLEY MARSHES IS ONE OF THE MOST BEAUTIFUL STRETCHES OF THE NORFOLK COASTLINE. THE VIEW ACROSS THE RECLAIMED SALT MARSHES TOWARDS THE SEA IS BREATHTAKING AND, IF YOU ARE INTERESTED IN BIRDWATCHING, THEN YOU WILL BE IN ORNITHOLOGICAL PARADISE.

Much of this walk takes in the geological phenomenon of Blakeney Point – a four-mile-long shingle spit, which is home to an amazing array of flora and fauna.

Cley itself has a proud seafaring history. The village now stands a mile from the sea, but in the Middle Ages Cley was an important trading port. These days the outstanding landmark is the 18th-century windmill, which stands at the edge of the marshes. At the top end of the village is the imposing 13th-century St Margaret's Church, which is found next to the village green. In the 13th century the harbour was just at the front of the church, demonstrating the coastline's fragile relationship with the sea.

The gradual decline of Cley from a major trading port to quiet coastal village dates back to the 14th century when plague decimated the population. Shortly after, a rogue landowner tried to unlawfully reclaim the marshes from the sea with devastating consequences for the land. The river silted up causing a cessation in local and overseas trade.

Six centuries later and the village is rediscovering itself as a destination for tourists, nature lovers and walkers. Within the village you will find a small number of independent shops and galleries. These include a fabulous delicatessen – Picnic Fayre – a bookshop, a well-stocked and high-quality gallery, a renowned smokehouse, a pottery and a number of tea shops – Cookes of Cley, West Cottage Cafe and the Garden Cafe, Cley Windmill, which serves three-course dinners – and a pub, the Three Swallows.

The area between the village and the sea is one of the most important nature reserves in Norfolk and has been designated an Area of Outstanding Natural Beauty. The nature reserve is also home to a recently built environmentally friendly visitor centre, incorporating an observation area.

The beach is mainly shingle and the waves can crash up the shoreline, making it less popular with beach-goers, but a haven for nature lovers, artists and fishermen.

While Cley might have long ago lost its pre-eminent status as a trading port, it still has an air of charm, mysticism and romance about it. Whether you are gazing out across the water from the steps of the magnificent church, imagining the ships rolling in with their loads of cotton and wool or looking back to the village across the marshes, with the soundtrack of gulls, terns and bitterns to keep you company, there is no doubt that this is one of the prettiest coastal views along this stretch of the UK's shoreline.

THE BASICS

Distance: 6 miles / 9.5km

Gradient: Mostly flat with one hill up to the church

Severity: Medium – the beach can make walking difficult

Approx. time to walk: 3½ hours

Stiles: None

Map: OS Explorer 251 (Norfolk Coast Central)

Path description: Minor road, grassy tracks, shingle and sand, shingle paths, marshland

Start point: The car park at Cley Village Hall (GR TG 047436)

Parking: The car park (free) at Cley Village Hall (NR25 7RG)

Dog friendly: Dogs must be kept on leads during the nesting season

Public toilets: At the Lifeboat House and at cafes in the village

Nearest food: Three tea rooms and a delicatessen that is great for picnic items

13 CLEY NEXT THE SEA

The Route

1. Park at the free car park behind the village hall in Cley village. As you leave the car park turn right onto the minor road leading back to the village and coast path. Where the tarmac road comes to an end, take the path to the right. This becomes very narrow as it goes past the backs of houses before emerging onto Cley High Street.

2. Turn left as you cross the road and after just a few metres turn right (just past the Custom House). This path brings you out in the courtyard of the iconic Cley Windmill. The path continues to the right of the windmill. Follow this path down to the marshes and then follow it along the sea bank right up to the beach.

3. You will be heading left along the beach. If the tide is out, you can follow the sand at the water's edge. However, if the tide is in, you will find it easier going if you walk at the edge of the marshes. There are many winding trails all leading in the same direction.

4. After one and a half miles of walking along the length of the shoreline you will come to the Watch House. This was built in the 19th century as a lookout for smugglers. It was then taken over by firstly the coast guard and then the girl guides. Now it is a holiday let.

5. Follow the shoreline back to the beach car park. Pick up Beach Road on your right, rather than the footpath, back to the main road. Cross over and you will see a marked footpath straight ahead. Follow this as it bends to the left. Eventually you will emerge onto Old Woman's Lane. Turn right and follow this road for about half a mile (800m). Take the second footpath on your right, and after approximately quarter of a mile turn left onto a minor road. Just 100 metres on and you will see

a footpath leading up to the church, with its magnificent views across the village and sea.

6. From here, retrace your steps to where the footpath entered the church yard. Turn left and follow the road back to the village hall car park.

If you have time, it is worth walking 600 metres towards Salthouse and visiting the Cley Nature Reserve.

14 GRESSENHALL TO BEETLEY

Gʀᴇssᴇɴʜᴀʟʟ ɪs ᴀ sᴍᴀʟʟ ᴠɪʟʟᴀɢᴇ ɪɴ ᴛʜᴇ Bʀᴇᴄᴋʟᴀɴᴅ ᴀʀᴇᴀ ᴏғ Nᴏʀғᴏʟᴋ. Iᴛ ɪs sɪᴛᴜᴀᴛᴇᴅ ɴᴇxᴛ ᴛᴏ ᴛʜᴇ Rɪᴠᴇʀ Nᴀʀ ᴀɴᴅ ɪs ᴛʜʀᴇᴇ ᴍɪʟᴇs ғʀᴏᴍ ᴛʜᴇ ᴍᴀʀᴋᴇᴛ ᴛᴏᴡɴ ᴏғ Eᴀsᴛ Dᴇʀᴇʜᴀᴍ ᴀɴᴅ 22 ᴍɪʟᴇs ғʀᴏᴍ Nᴏʀᴡɪᴄʜ.

The agricultural nature of this part of the country is still clear to the visitor. Much of the land is arable, although the crop diversity is much greater than in earlier times. Gressenhall Farm and Workhouse, Norfolk's museum of rural life, is well worth a visit as it is both a working farm and a reminder of how our own past.

The museum is housed in a former workhouse, which actually remained in operation until 1948, providing food, work and a roof for destitute single people and families. The original workhouse was built much earlier – in 1777 – but underwent a number of extensions in the 19th century. Alongside the workhouse, visitors can also see a replica 1930s village, complete with traditional businesses such as a blacksmith's forge and an old-style post office.

The farm, which is a working farm, houses a number of rare breed animals, such as Norfolk Horn Sheep and Suffolk Punch horses. If you have time and energy after the walk, the farm has a number of trails, which take you through some fantastic gardens and around the fascinating farm.

This walk, with the museum, feels like a real step back in time as you follow virtually empty country roads, verdant field edges and old tracks that have been trodden by centuries of farm workers.

This walk takes you along part of the Nar Valley Way, through beautifully preserved woodland, well-maintained farmland and along some pretty (and quiet) country lanes.

THE BASICS

Distance: 6½ miles / 10.5km
Gradient: Mostly flat with one section of gently undulating hills
Approx. time to walk: 3 hours
Stiles: None
Map: OS Explorer 238 (Dereham & Aylsham)
Path description: Country lanes, farm tracks, grassy verges and footpaths
Start point: Gressenhall Farm and Workhouse (GR TF 974169)
Parking: At Gressenhall Farm and Workhouse (NR20 4DR)
Dog friendly: Dogs should be kept on a lead near livestock and on roads.
Public toilets: At Gressenhall Farm and Workhouse
Nearest food: At the museum, and at the post office and store, one mile into the walk

The Route

1. Leave the car park and turn right on to the B1146. Take the next right, which is the Nar Valley Way, one of Norfolk's prettiest long-distance footpaths. This takes you past a copse and then through Gressenhall itself. When you reach the Swan Inn turn right, past more houses, until you reach a crossroads. Turn left here, following signs for the Nar Valley Way.

2. After about 100 yards (91m), take the footpath to your right, still the Nar Valley Way. This narrow path lies between tall hedges and is like a green tunnel in summer and spring. It widens eventually and, after about three-quarters of a mile, emerges on to a track called Stoney Lane. Turn left, still following signs for the Nar Valley Way, and walk for another three-quarters of a mile until you reach a plantation of tall pine trees. Turn left, leaving the Nar Valley Way. The foundations of the deserted village of Bittering Parva are to the right.

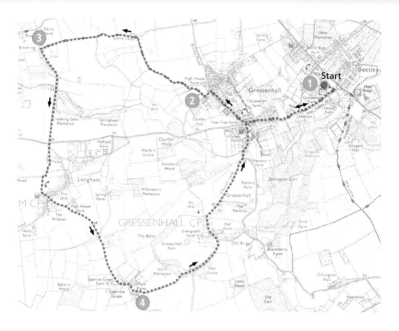

3. When you reach a crossroads and Ostrich House, follow the lane towards Longham. At the next fork bear right, past Longham Village Hall Sports and Social Club, and walk along the wide street. Turn sharp left at the White Horse at Longham. Walk down a hill, then up the other side, with pretty views across working land to your right.

4. Once you have passed the barn conversions and a pair of silos, turn left at Park Farm Cottages, and walk for about three-quarters of a mile, until you reach a junction. Turn left here, passing Hall Farm on your right and Evergreen Farm on your left. You are now on Church Lane, a quiet country road that will take you back to the Nar Valley Way. As you reach the Nar Valley Way, by the Post Office and General Store, turn right and retrace your steps back to the workhouse museum.

AYLSHAM IS A NORFOLK MARKET TOWN, LYING IN THE HEART OF RURAL COUNTRYSIDE ON THE BANKS OF THE BURE RIVER AND WITHIN EASY ACCESS OF BOTH THE FASCINATING WATERWAYS OF THE NORFOLK BROADS AND THE MAGNIFICENT BEAUTY OF THE NORTH NORFOLK COAST.

The town is also home to the Bure Valley Railway, a narrow-gauge railway offering 18-mile round trips through the stunning Bure Valley to Wroxham. With its population of 6,000, Aylsham is a genuine market town, with two general weekly markets, two monthly farmers' markets and several speciality markets throughout the year. The markets date back to 1519, when Henry VIII granted a market and annual fair to be held on 12 March, the eve of the Feast of St Gregory.

Today Aylsham is renowned as a champion of local artisan foods and drink, but from the 14th century to the 18th century most of its wealth and prosperity was thanks to the wool and cloth trade. The glorious Georgian houses that line the marketplace are a sign that Aylsham was home to many a wealthy trader.

One other feature of note in Aylsham is the 14th century church of St Michael which dominates views across the town. It is said the church was funded by John O'Gaunt – the third son of Edward III and uncle to Richard III – and he is featured on the town sign. John O'Gaunt was lord of the manor from 1372 and while there is no evidence that he ever lived in the town, his patronage would have meant substantial tax benefits for the local population.

Aylsham itself is just two miles from the site of the Roman settlement Venta Icenorum, which is said to have been the capital city of Norfolk before Norwich was founded. Excavations have thrown up several kilns, showing that Aylsham and the surrounding area was part of a large Roman industrial area.

Since Norman times, the area surrounding Aylsham has always attracted royalty and their relatives. National Trust properties Felbrigg Hall, Mannington and Wolterton are all stately homes within easy reach of Aylsham, while the magnificent Jacobean stately home Blicking Hall – which was home to Anne

Boleyn, the unfortunate second wife of Henry VIII – is now home to the annual Aylsham Country Show. The well-attended show is held on the parkland surrounding the hall and the gardens host night-time star-gazing events.

THE BASICS

Distance: 6 miles / 9.5km

Gradient: Mostly flat, although there are steep steps as you cross the Marriott's Way early in the walk

Severity: Quite easy

Approx. time to walk: 3 hours

Stiles: Three

Map: OS Explorer 238 (Dereham & Aylsham)

Path description: Road, marked trails, fields and footpaths; may be muddy at times

Start point: Buttlands car park, Mill Road, Aylsham (GR TG 191266)

Parking: Buttlands car park, Mill Road (free) (NR11 6DU)

Dog friendly: Yes, but be aware of livestock and nesting birds

Public toilets: A number of restaurants and cafes in the centre of Aylsham

Nearest food: There are a number of coffee shops, tea rooms and cafes around the Market Square

The Route

1. Head south out of the car park to Mill Road and turn right. At the end of the road, turn left into Cawston Road. About 100 metres along the road turn left along a track signposted public footpath, to Stonegate Lane, which begins life as Jewel's Lane. Continue along the track and path. Take the steps and cross over the Marriott's Way, and across the main B1145.

2. Cross the road and almost immediately cross a stile straight ahead. Take the continuing field-edge path and at a field boundary head directly across the field. Cross a stile into the next field, ignore the more trodden left-hand path and continue straight ahead, slightly to the right, crossing a footbridge over a dyke, and then head for the field corner. Cross the next stile and then turn left along the lane.

3. Pass Stonegate Farm and then turn right along a track. Ignore the track which goes to the left; instead follow the grass track straight ahead. At the end of this track, turn right. You will see a concrete area on your right; just past this, where the track veers left, head directly across the field towards a gap in the far hedge. At the road, cross and veer left along a track. After a short distance, turn right before a wooden fence and walk along a field boundary with woodland on your left. Continue along a track which turns left and then right along the edge of the woodland. The track turns left again; here take the path that veers to the right off the track through the edge of the woodland.

4. At the bottom of the railway embankment, turn right along the path that runs just below the embankment. At the gap before a mound, turn left and then right. You are now on the Marriott's Way.

5. Continue along the Marriott's Way for approximately three-quarters of a mile, crossing a track and continuing. Pass through the next gates over a track. Where the path crosses the road, after the gate, turn left and then immediately right to join Green Lane.

6. This straight road takes you between an avenue of trees and hedges towards St Michael's Place – the former Aylsham hospital. The path veers and takes you past Manor Farm. Pass the farmhouse and go through a gate. At the end of the road, turn

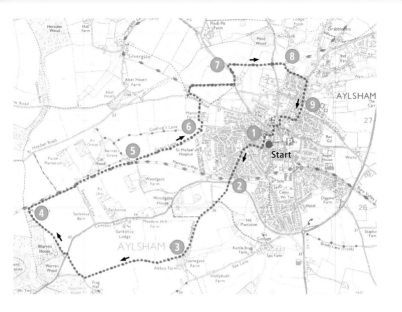

left and take two right-hand turns taking you across a stile and into a wide grassed avenue.

7. You are now on the ancient Weavers' Way, heading towards Aylsham Old Hall, dated 1686, in the distance. Exit the grassed avenue by the gate and turn left onto the road. You follow the grass road verge for a short distance uphill before turning right to rejoin the Weavers' Way.

8. Pass through a gate and head along the Weavers' Way, eventually walking over a bridge, then under an old railway bridge and then continue over three further bridges. Follow the path under the next bridge and straight ahead through a gate. Cross the road bridge, but beware of traffic, as there is no footpath along this road.

9. Cross two bridges – to the left at the second bridge is a good view of the late 18th-century Aylsham Mill. Turn right into New Road and where the road bends to the right, pass Ash House on the left and turn left into Abbott's Close. Take the next right turn into Town Lane, which emerges opposite the Methodist Hall. Here turn right and then left into Red Lion Street, signed Town Centre. Turn right through the Market Place surrounded by 17th and 18th-century properties. (Pic 5) At the Black Boys inn, cross into Hungate Street ahead and shortly turn right into Unicorn Yard. Continue along the path, turning left into the car park and back to the start of the walk.

WHILE NORFOLK IS KNOWN FOR ITS COASTLINE AND COUNTRYSIDE, A WALKING TOUR OF THE COUNTY WOULD NOT BE COMPLETE WITH A VISIT TO THE CAPITAL CITY, NORWICH. OUR WALK WINDS ALONG BOTH SIDES OF THE RIVER WENSUM, TAKING IN MANY OF THE OLD AND MODERN ARCHITECTURAL SITES OF THE CITY ALONG THE WAY.

Part of the charm of Norwich lies in the fact that it is geographically separated from much of the UK. With its rows of independent shops, medieval street patterns and imposing castle and defensive wall, Norwich has escaped the 'sameness' that is creeping over so many of the UK's cities.

Despite its position to the far east of the country, history shows us that Norwich has always played an important role in the nation's history. From medieval times through to the Industrial Revolution, Norwich was England's second city. The arrival of the Normans heralded the start of a prolonged period of wealth in the city, reflected in the range of historic buildings that still stand today – Norwich Castle and Norwich Cathedral are two fine examples.

With the Industrial Revolution that took place from 1850 onwards, Norwich's status among cities changed. As other towns grew into cities on the back of the coal, iron and steel trade, Norwich, with its reliance on agriculture and brewing, began to take more of a back seat, avoiding the huge urban sprawl that occurred in places such as Liverpool, Sheffield, Manchester and Birmingham. However, two industries that hark back to the Industrial Revolution still survive and thrive in Norwich today – boot and shoe making and Colman's Mustard.

These days, Norwich is a city renowned for its literary scene – it is one of only two English cities to be a UNESCO City of Literature – and all year round there are festivals, book clubs, author readings and literature festivals to celebrate its rich cultural traditions.

For shopaholics, the Lanes, which was voted the 2014 Shopping Street of the Year, has a range of quirky, independent shops offering lifestyle, fashion and art against a backdrop of narrow alleys and historic buildings. The area also houses galleries, cafes, eclectic entertainment venues and any number of atmospheric pubs, many offering craft beer from the numerous micro-brewers who work in and around the city.

Norwich, which sits on the River Wensum, is two hours from London by train and the Norfolk Broads and the beautiful Norfolk coastline are a short trip away. It is a compact city, easy to navigate and walk around; but be warned: although Norfolk has a reputation for flatness, Norwich is actually one of the hilliest cities in England.

THE BASICS

Distance: 5 miles / 8km

Gradient: Mostly flat, but a few steep city hills

Severity: Quite easy

Approx. time to walk: 2½ hours

Stiles: None

Map: The best option is a street map from the Tourist Information Centre or an app for a mobile device (available from www.visitnorwich.co.uk)

Path description: Roads and footpaths

Start point: Westwick Street car park (GR TG 225089)

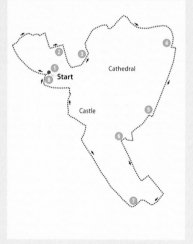

Parking: Westwick Street car park (NR2 4SZ) (currently £3.90 for three hours)

Dog friendly: Yes, but must be on lead at all times

Public toilets: Throughout the city

Nearest food: A wide range of food outlets on the way

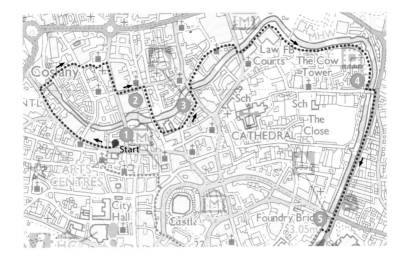

The Route

1. Leave the car park and turn left into Westwick Street. Turn left into New Mills Yard. Go straight ahead to cross New Mills Bridge, then turn right to follow the path. Turn right over the next bridge. Continue ahead until you reach the T-junction with the main road. Turn left onto the pavement heading uphill. Opposite the Mash Tun pub, merge left onto Charing Cross. At the traffic lights turn left into Duke Street.

   Cross over the river and on the left you'll pass a beautiful old Victorian building which now houses Norwich University of the Arts. Soon afterwards cross the road via a pedestrian crossing with lights and continue down Colegate.

2. When you reach the crossroads with St George's Street, turn right. Cross over St George's Bridge and go ahead past Norwich Technical Institute on the left. Immediately after this, turn left through the bollards, and pass under an archway into an old courtyard. Follow the path turning left and then right to emerge out into a car park alongside the river.

3. Continue along with the river on your left. At The Ribs of Beef public house, follow the path running to the right to reach a T-junction with the main road. Turn left and follow the road over Fye Bridge and then cross the road to turn right down Fishergate. At the end of the road, turn right over Whitefriars Bridge. Cross the road and go down the flight of steps to the riverside path. Follow the gravel path as it winds through the small grass area and then keep left to cross over the next bridge. At the far side of the bridge turn left down the steps and then left again to continue along the river bank.

4. Immediately opposite a tower on the right-hand bank, turn left up a fenced alleyway. At the end of the alley bear right, then turn left up the flight of steps to reach the road. Turn right onto the pavement and follow it along a walled section. As you reach the pedestrian crossing, turn right to cross Bishops Bridge. After just a few paces cross the road and turn left down a paved alleyway (note that the gates through this section are locked at dusk). The path emerges to

become a riverside path. Continue through the gates and follow this path through another gate and over a small footbridge.

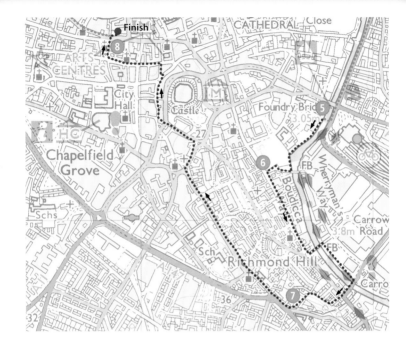

5. Go up the steps to pass through the patio garden of the Compleat Angler and then turn left over Foundry Bridge. At the lights cross over to the right and then follow the right fork in the pavement to pass by Norwich Sea Cadets training ship, TS Lord Nelson.

6. Pass alongside a number of cafes and restaurants on the left, then turn left up a few steps before turning right to cross over Lady Julian Bridge. Follow the path ahead and then merge onto the pavement alongside St Ann Lane. At the T-junction turn left onto King Street. Continue to the end of this road. At the end, turn left over another suspension bridge. After crossing, turn sharp right to return to the river bank and then turn left to follow the river path. Keep left at the fork, heading uphill. At the top of the footpath turn right to cross the final bridge on the walk. Turn right into King Street, then turn left up a few steps onto Southgate Lane.

7. Continue uphill along the walled footpath. At the top turn left and follow the wider vehicle lane continuing uphill. At the T-junction turn right onto Bracondale, then after just a short distance keep right into Ber Street. Continue ahead along Ber Street. At the junction, cross via the pedestrian crossings left and then right, to go down the pedestrian walkway.

   At the bottom of the hill cross over the pedestrian crossing and then fork right down White Lion Street. Keep right to pass the Castle Mall entrance. Continue down Castle Street.

8. Cross London Road and go down Swan Lane, then turn left into Bedford Street. At the crossroads, go straight ahead into Lobster Lane. Continue ahead on Pottergate. Immediately after passing The Birdcage, turn right in front of St Gregory's Church and follow the footpath, St Gregory's Alley.

   Turn left into St Benedict's Street but before you reach the traffic lights cross to the right-hand pavement and then continue ahead to reach the lights. A few paces before the lights, turn right onto a footpath. Follow the pavement alongside the main road. Immediately after the retail park, you will see Westwick Street car park where the walk began.

Strumpshaw Fen and the surrounding area is an absolute haven for wildlife and a beautiful place for those who just enjoy a good walk in interesting and diverse countryside. This walk takes you past the Fen, into the open countryside and woodlands.

Strumpshaw itself is a small village with no more than 500 residents, but a surprisingly busy community feel. The village boasts a steam museum, dedicated to the preservation and showcasing of steam engines, a conservation pit, Railway Wood – a wildlife corridor for birds, mammals and insects – plus two pubs, a livery yard and a post office, which also houses a wine shop specialising in wine from the Languedoc region of France.

While Strumpshaw village is worth a look around, the focus of this walk is the Fen and the surrounding countryside. Our walk starts from the car park of the RSPB reserve and, although the walk does not go into the reserve, it is certainly worth a visit while you are there. It is one of the best places to see and enjoy the wildlife of the Norfolk Broads and the walk itself passes a diverse and rich variety of habitat, from orchid-rich meadows to woodlands, reed beds and fen.

At various times of the year, you will see marsh harriers, bitterns, kingfishers, bearded tits, Chinese water deer, water voles, otters and the beautiful swallowtail butterflies. Each season brings a different experience and a different set of visitors.

In spring, the air is filled with birdsong as they compete to establish territory and find a mate. The songs of the spring migrants include the reed warblers, the universally recognisable sound of the cuckoo and the drumming noise of lesser and greater spotted woodpeckers.

Summer sees the young fledgling birds making their first flights, but this is really when flora takes centre stage. The meadows come alive with wild flowers, including six different species of wild orchid. It is also the time to spot butterflies and up to twenty different types of dragonfly.

Autumn is a time for preparation for migration and you will often spot ospreys fishing as they linger on their southward migration. This is also the best time of year to catch the heart-stopping sight of a kingfisher – usually no more than an electric blue and orange flash.

The bittern is the star of the show in winter. This little bird with a larger than life 'boom' lives among the reed beds and, as the vegetation thins, a lucky walker might catch a glimpse of the almost prehistoric-looking bird.

You will also be forgiven if you jump out of your skin the first time you hear the song of Cetti's warbler – these little brown and grey birds are hard to see, but the explosive nature of their call is unmistakeable and unforgettable.

THE BASICS

Distance: 6 miles / 9.5km

Gradient: Some undulations in the ground but only gentle inclines

Severity: Quite easy

Approx. time to walk: 2½ hours

Stiles: None

Map: OS Explorer OL40 (The Broads)

Path description: Tarmac road, marked trails, field edges and footpaths

Start point: Strumpshaw Fen RSPB (GR TG 340065)

Parking: Strumpshaw Fen RSPB car park (free) (NR13 4HS)

Dog friendly: Yes, but keep on lead when on the RSPB site

Public toilets: At the RSPB centre at the start and finish of the walk

Refreshments: You can buy a cup of tea or coffee at the RSPB centre

The Route

1. Leave the car park at the southerly end, keeping the bird reserve on your right. Follow the road as it mirrors the route of the railway line towards Buckenham. This is a quiet, single-track road but do be aware that cars can appear.

2. Cross the railway track at the pedestrian crossing. You are now on Station Road, still heading towards Buckenham. There is a conservation area to your right and open fields to your left. After approximately three-quarters of a mile you will see a second pedestrian crossing over the railway line. Take this, taking care to look out for trains, and turn right to follow the path around the edge of the field.

3. As you reach the end of the fields, you will emerge onto a tarmac road. To your right is the tiny Buckenham Station. Turn left, away from the station, and follow the road, past the Second World War lookout building, and then a further 100 metres on, take the marked footpath across the field towards St Nicholas Church.

4. Turn left and go past the line of farm cottages. At the junction, turn right and follow the quiet road down the hill. You will see farm buildings on your right, but before you reach them, there is a bridle path between two hedge rows on your left. Take this, as it goes up a gentle slope. At

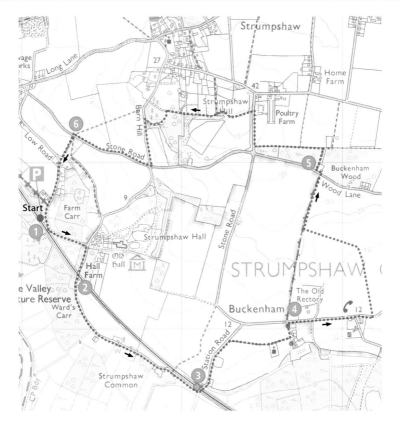

the top of the hill, turn right, heading towards a white house. This is Squirrel View Cottage.

5. Turn left onto the road and after just a few metres, turn right following a footpath. This brings you to Buckenham Road. Turn left and follow this past a cluster of houses. Before you reach the next left-hand turn in the road, you will see a footpath leading to Strumpshaw Hill. This is a recently constructed wildlife area built on a landfill site. A footpath runs around its perimeter. Take the track and after a few metres turn left. The footpath bears left and then right, before turning right again. Follow the track for approximately 400 metres and then leave the landfill site and join Mill Hill Road. Cross the road (this is now Stone Road) and join the grass track that runs along the field, parallel to the road. At the end of this field turn left and follow the tarmac road past the Steam Museum and the livery yard.

6. Turn right when you come to Low Road and follow the road back to the car park.

18 CARLTON BROAD

This walk, taking in parts of Carlton Broad and Oulton Broad, spans two counties. It starts and ends in Norfolk, at the Waveney River Centre, but much of the walk is in Suffolk. You start the walk with a short ferry ride.

The Broads stretch over more than 300 square kilometres, encompassing parts of east Norfolk and north Suffolk. Carlton Marshes Nature Reserve is part of this intensive system of man-made, navigable waterways. It is also famous as Britain's largest nationally protected wetland, with all the accompanying diversity of species you would expect.

The Broads were first created when man started digging for peat, but soon the potential as a means of transporting goods was realised and so the area turned into a network of communities living and working on and around the Broads.

Man's influence has created an incredibly diverse habitat – over the course of the walk you will see grazing land, reed beds, fenland and marshes. This in turn attracts a myriad of wildlife so this is also a twitcher's haven. Marsh harriers, barn owls, bitterns and many warbler species are the most popular feathered visitors and inhabitants although you might also see water voles and otters as well as a variety of deer.

The watery landscape means that you will also see parties of schoolchildren pond-dipping for insects and it is worth stopping for a few minutes to peer beneath the surface and watch the underwater world as it goes about its business.

As you begin your walk, across to the left you will have beautiful views beyond the reeds across Oulton Broad. Oulton Broad, thought to be the remnant of medieval peat cutting, is the most southern of the Norfolk Broads. It is a popular tourist and sporting centre and you are likely to see everything from powerboat racing to sailing, rowing and canoeing. On the far bank you will be able to see the beautiful red-brick buildings of the Old Maltings. Once a key part of the brewing industry, today the buildings are in use as residential apartments.

This six-mile circular might be flat, but with a ferry ride, reed beds, a nature reserve and plenty of bustling boat life, it is far from boring.

THE BASICS

Distance: 5¾ miles / 9.25km

Gradient: Nearly all flat

Severity: Quite easy

Approx. time to walk: 2½ hours

Stiles: Five

Map: OS Explorer OL40 (The Broads)

Path description: Marked trails and footpaths, one slightly boggy part by the river

Start point: At the Burgh St Peter Ferry at Waveney River Centre (GR TM 491934)

Parking: Waveney River Centre, Burgh St Peter (NR34 0DD)

Dog friendly: Yes, dogs are allowed on the ferry. On the walk be aware of animals and nesting birds

Public toilets: At start of walk at the Waveney River Centre

Nearest food: The Waveney Inn and The Waveney River Centre Cafe both serve food and there is a well-stocked grocery store within the centre

*The ferry service runs on demand throughout the year, subject to tidal and weather conditions. It can be summoned on 07500–571232. At the time of writing (2016) the fares are £2 single, £3 same day return or £10 return for a group of four. See waveneyrivercentre.co.uk/carlton-burghstpeter-ferry.

18 CARLTON BROAD

The Route

1. From the ferry landing take the path right along the top of the river bank for 130 metres. Pass the end of the new flood defence bank and take the temporary steps down the bank onto the grass field. There is a new dyke to your left; walk parallel with this. If it is very wet, take the thin strip of drier land along the bottom of the new dyke.

2. After 200 metres you cross over a culvert. Keep straight ahead to the path, which is on slightly raised ground. Ignore the path to your right and keep straight ahead on the slightly raised ground. Follow the track over another culvert then left towards a double gate structure.

3. Do not go through the gates but bear right beside them. You are now on a diverted path with large red signs showing the way ahead. The diverted path will eventually bring you out onto a track. Follow this track for half a mile to the Suffolk Wildlife Trust car park.

4. Enter the car park and turn left across it to pick up a surfaced footpath running between an arable field and a dyke. Following the path, you come to a junction where the path turns left. Ignore this and continue straight ahead to join an enclosed path leading to a stile into a grass field. Cross the stile and follow the field boundary towards Ivy House Country Hotel. Cross the lane via the stiles and continue. Following the worn path around the field edges, you will come to another stile leading into a holiday park.

5. Continue straight ahead and take the gap between hedges. You emerge onto a lane. Keep straight ahead for a few metres then pass through a gap in the wire fence on your left. Follow the path through the short stretch of woodland until you emerge into a grassy area. Walk to the end of the grass and turn right to follow a thin path which leads left to join a tarmac path.

6. Take a left turn over a timber bridge to enter Nicholas Everitt Park. Keep straight ahead until you reach the tarmac path. Here you pass in front of Lowestoft Rowing Club boathouse (pic 3) and slipways. Turn left and follow the path around the edge of the park against the water front. This will eventually bring you out onto the Boulevard, Oulton Broad.

7. You will now retrace your steps through part of the journey, passing back through Nicholas Everitt Park and Lowestoft Rowing Club and slipways. Turn right beside the slipway then take the first left turn. At a junction of paths cross over the timber footbridge and turn immediately right. Follow this thin path round to the right until you come to a gate onto a lane. Do not go through the gate but turn left onto the

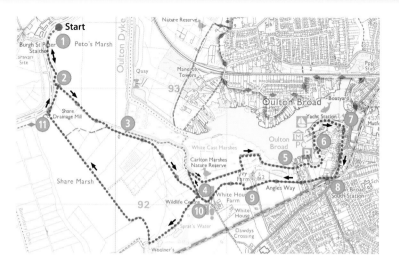

long area of grass. Walk to the end of this and follow the worn path through a thin strip of woodland to a lane.

8. Turn right and at the next right-hand bend take the public footpath straight ahead. This is signed the Angles Way. Follow the path through the holiday park. Leave the park over a stile to enter a grass field. The worn path takes you back to the access lane to Ivy House Country Hotel. Cross over the lane via the stiles and continue along the edge of the grass field.

9. At the end of the field cross over the stile into an enclosed footpath. Follow this to come to a junction with a path leading to the right. Keep straight ahead to follow the now made-up path between a fence and a ditch.

10. Cross the Suffolk Wildlife Trust car park, to join the track leading out over the marshes. Pass through the gate and immediately take the left-hand path, with a temporary sign saying Alternative Route to Ferry. This path skirts the edge of the marsh, and is joined by another coming in from the right just before passing through a gate. Pass through this and the next gate to emerge onto a path between reed beds. Keep straight ahead to a crossroads of paths. Take the right-hand track, opposite the reserve entrance. This track heads out across the marsh, parallel with some power lines.

11. After three-quarters of a mile you will reach a sign indicating a right turn over a bridge through a gate. The path leads straight out over a field. As you near the new flood defence bank there is a temporary sign indicating the ferry to the left. You have now rejoined your route out from the Waveney River Centre. Turn left and track back to the river then right to the ferry.

19 WEAVERS' WAY – FELMINGHAM

THE ANCIENT WEAVERS' WAY HAS BEEN TRODDEN BY TRAVELLERS FOR CENTURIES. IT WAS ONE OF A NETWORK OF ROUTES FOR PEDESTRIAN SALESMEN, PEOPLE ON HORSEBACK AND CARTS FULL OF GRAIN, WOOL AND NUMEROUS OTHER COMMODITIES AS THEY TRAVELLED BETWEEN THE TOWNS AND VILLAGES ACROSS NORFOLK.

It was named after the cloth trade that was one of the main industries, alongside the production of grain, in Norfolk before the Industrial Revolution. Today the route is hugely popular with walkers and hikers. The entire Weavers' Way is 56 miles long and runs from Cromer to Great Yarmouth, passing through the villages and towns of Hanworth, Aylsham, North Walsham, Potter Heigham and Halvergate before crossing marshes at Berney Arms and joining with the Wherryman's Way.

At Cromer, Weavers' Way links with the Norfolk Coastal Path, while at the seaside holiday resort of Great Yarmouth it joins the Angles Way. Together with the Peddars Way, these routes make a circuit of long-distance walks around Norfolk.

This six-mile walk along part of the Weavers' Way takes in the village of Felmingham, the market town of North Walsham and a mixed countryside landscape of fields, heathlands, open grasslands, old pathways and woods full of native trees.

The first and very last section of the walk is along the disused railway track, which was part of the Midland and Great Northern Railway. The railway opened in 1883, part of the explosion of railway activity across the UK as the Industrial Revolution opened up parts of the country for purposes of trade and tourism. Passenger services were withdrawn on the line in 1959 and now the old track is all that remains – an evocative reminder of the past and a good walking track these days.

At Stump Cross, we are reminded of events that took place long before the Industrial Revolution. Stump Cross is a memorial commemorating the Peasants' Revolt of 1381. The most famous tales surrounding the Peasants' Revolt focus on the rebel army led by Wat Tyler, a roof tiler from Kent. But across England ordinary people were so incensed by the actions of the monarch, Richard II, that localised militia rose up in an open revolt against the royal household, after the king and his chancellor raised the poll tax – a tax on every adult person in England – from fourpence to one shilling, the equivalent of two weeks' wages.

Across the country, workers rose up in a strong display of their anger. The Tyler-led march to London by workers from Kent is well chronicled but a less well-known part of that movement saw peasants across East Anglia join in the bloody protests. Peasants attacked Cambridge University, killing many royal officials, and at Stump Cross and the surrounding countryside a rebel army rose up to challenge the royal tax collectors. The people's army was defeated by a royal regiment in a conflict known as the Battle of North Walsham.

THE BASICS

Distance: 6 miles / 9.5km
Gradient: Some slight inclines
Severity: Quite easy
Approx. time to walk: 3 hours
Stiles: None
Map: OS Explorer 252 (Norfolk Coast East)
Path description: Road, marked trails, fields and footpaths
Start point: Weavers' Way car park, Felmingham (GR TG 250286)
Parking: Weaver's Way car park, Felmingham (free) (NR28 0LL)
Dog friendly: Yes, if they can manage the stiles, but be aware of animals and nesting birds
Public toilets: None at start, but public toilets in North Walsham
Nearest food: North Walsham has a range of cafes and shops for provisions on route

The Route

1. Walk from the car park through the gate onto the disused railway line. Turn left and follow the route of the old railway line. This is also part of the Weavers' Way. The disused railway station is on your right.

2. Follow the course of the railway line for the next mile and a quarter. You will travel through woods and alongside arable fields. The route will also take you over two bridges. Eventually you pass through a gate, cross the road and go through the next gate. The Weavers' Way continues, for just over another mile, to another gate and Station Road, on the edge of the market town of North Walsham.

3. Turn right and you will soon come to a mini-roundabout. Go straight for about quarter of a mile, along Millfield Road ,until you come to a T-junction, where you turn right.

4. Continue along this road until you reach two water towers. You will find the remains of Stump Cross on the right-hand side of the road.

5. Take the waymarked public footpath to your right. This follows a track for a short while before opening out into a large field.

6. Continue along this path to the corner of the field, where the path meets the field edge and runs along the left-hand side of a hedge.

7. Where the path joins a track, take the waymarked public footpath straight ahead which crosses the middle of the field that leads to the woods. At the field edge, continue along the track into the woods. When you come to a dip in the track look to your right where you will see the ruins of Strawberry Hall.

8. Continue along the track until you reach a gate. Take the footpath immediately to the right, which heads diagonally across a field. Pass through the hedge, across another field to a track. Here you turn left, then after just 80 metres turn right to cross the next field at the public footpath waymarker.

9. When you reach the road, turn right. Opposite the white cottage take the public footpath that crosses the field to the left. Pass through the gap in the hedge and cross the field to a minor lane.

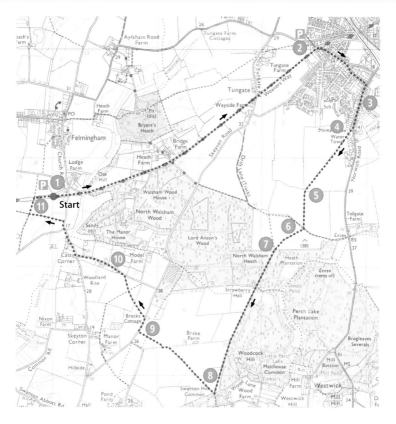

10. Turn left, then at the next T-junction turn right. Continue along this road to the road junction; just past here you will see a signed public footpath on the left. Take this footpath until you reach a crossroads of paths. Turn right and cross the field.

11. At the hedge line step, you will find a set of steep steps leading to Felmingham Cutting Local Nature Reserve. You are now back on the disused railway track and Weavers' Way. Turn right and in 200 metres you will be back at the car park on the left.

20 WROXHAM

Wroxham is often referred to as the Capital of the Broads, an accolade that is attributable to the proliferation of boating yards and holiday excursion centres that can be found in the town.

The area around Wroxham Bridge is a local shopping centre with the firm of Roys of Wroxham at its heart – the store has been known since the 1930s as the 'world's largest village store'.

Wroxham and Hoveton became the starting point for visitors to the Broads in the late 19th century when the expansion of the railway line across England made access to the area easier. The East Norfolk railway arrived in Wroxham and Hoveton between 1874 and 1876 and this walk follows parts of that line.

Wroxham and its close neighbour Hoveton sit on an elevated position above the River Bure, between Belaugh Broad to the west and Wroxham Broad to the east or south east. (pic 2)

The Broads consist of more than 125 miles of navigable lock-free waterways set in beautiful countryside. The landscape is a mixture of marshland fields, feathery reed beds and tangled woodlands and is a magical place to escape and wander for a few hours.

It is easy to forget that the Broads are man-made and not a natural phenomenon, but their history dates back to the 12th century, a time when the local population was relatively dense for England at that period. Materials for fuel were becoming scarce because the woodlands had been cleared for agriculture, and a new type of fuel was needed.

It was at this time that peat was discovered to be a useful alternative fuel source and so centuries of peat digging in the area began. It is estimated that over a period of 200 years, 900 million cubic feet of peat was extracted.

From the 14th to the 16th century, the peat holes filled with water and from the 1700s onwards the Broads became an important channel for commerce and commerce. Norwich was the second largest city in Norwich and many of its tradable goods of wool, weaving and agriculture were transported by boat through the Broads to Great Yarmouth and then overseas.

Of course, that trade has ceased now, and the main business is tourism, but it takes very little imagination to picture a time when the Broads was a bustling centre of trade and commerce.

THE BASICS

Distance: 6 miles / 9.5km

Gradient: Some slight inclines

Severity: Quite easy

Approx. time to walk: 3 hours

Stiles: Two

Map: OS Explorer OL40 (The Broads)

Path description: Road, marked trails, fields, river paths and footpaths

Start point: Hoveton and Wroxham Station (GR TG 303184)

Parking: Hoveton and Wroxham Station (NR12 8UR) (free)

Dog friendly: Yes, if they can manage the stiles, but be aware of animals and nesting birds

Public toilets: At the station

Nearest food: There is a cafe at the station, but within Wroxham there are a range of cafes, restaurants and public houses

20 WROXHAM

The Route

1. Leave Hoveton and Wroxham Station and pass over the footbridge, following signs to the Bure Valley Railway. Head towards the station and pass behind it to join the Bure Valley Path. The path follows the narrow-gauge railway and you may see the steam train that runs between here and Aylsham.

2. The path opens out into onto open countryside, and you will soon pass a crossing keeper's cottage and cross a road. Stay on the path until you pass under a red-brick railway bridge.

3. Once under the bridge, turn left and take the steep flight of steps to join the road.

4. Turn right along the country road. At the junction where there is a small wooded green; take the right fork and head along the road.

5. Eventually the road bends sharply right. At this point you need to turn left and take the footpath going left. (There is a bridleway going right, but ignore that.) The footpath crosses fields and passes through kissing gates. Eventually you emerge into Coltishall village, opposite the village shop and post office.

6. Cross the road to the King's Head Inn car park. Cross the car park diagonally left and take the small footbridge which takes you to Coltishall Lower Common.

7. At the end of the Common there is a brick and flint wall and a road heading left. Take the road and follow it for a few minutes before turning right past The Old Rectory into Anchor Street. Walk to the end of Anchor Street, then climb over two stiles into a field. Take the right-hand footpath through the meadow, keeping the hedge on your left and the River Bure on your right. You will cross meadows and pass through two gates.

8. Eventually you will come to a stile into a small lane or loke. Walk along the loke past a converted barn and a flint house.